The FEARLESS ENTREPRENEURS

Fear Less; Be More

created by

LYNDA SUNSHINE WEST

Dedicated to all the entrepreneurs out there who are making this planet a better place.

Foreword by
Erik "Mr. Awesome" Sv
Women Action Takers™ F

San Diego, California

Women Action Takers™ Publishing

www.womenactiontakers.com

ebook ISBN: 978-1-7348759-3-5

Paperback ISBN: 978-1-7348759-2-8

Editorial services by Kristy Boyd Johnson of Turtle Sea Books

Cover Design by Ryanzzzz

Printed in the United States of America

Table of Contents

See yourself through the eyes of others, for others see the real you.
~Lynda Sunshine West

FOREWORD

by Erik "Mr. Awesome" Swanson, Founder
Habitude Warrior Conference

On December 12th, 1997, I had the pleasure of giving myself a gift. A gift of success and a gift that would ultimately change the course of my life in such a profound way. The funny thing is that I had no idea at the time. You see, this was the day in my life in which I had the amazing opportunity to meet the one and only Brian Tracy!

I would be remiss if I didn't tell you that I truly had NO idea who Brian Tracy was at the time. A friend of mine had suggested to me that I should check out this seminar happening in the Denver area. Three problems that I saw right off the bat: #1) I had never been to a business seminar in my life; #2) this particular event cost about $799.00; #3) and lastly, I didn't live in Denver. I lived in Austin, Texas at the time.

I'm sure you could see some of my dilemmas forming. But, I had to find out why my friend was so adamant about me attending this event. He truly believed in me and believed that if I started to surround myself with great leaders and brilliant thinkers of our day, such as Brian

Tracy, then I could apply those same principles to grow into my own success.

After days and days of thinking about attending, the biggest issue kept rearing its ugly head. There wasn't any way I could possibly afford to attend this event at the price of the tickets. I told my friend, "I simply can't afford it!" He suggested to me that he would pick up 1/2 of the cost of the ticket for me to attend. My answer promptly to him was, "I can't even afford 1/2 of the ticket!" I explained to him that I had a lot of credit card debt at the time and I'm trying to work my way out of that. He asked me what the amount of debt I had. After I told him the amount, without missing a beat, he proclaimed, "So, what's another $400 on your card?"

He was right! It was time for me to take the bull by the horns! Well, at least one horn since I was only paying for 1/2 of the ticket to this event. But, seriously, it was truly time for me to give myself permission to succeed. Enough with those days of struggling and struggling by trying to figure it all out by myself. If a good friend of mine who I truly trusted and who was very successful was offering to take a chance on me, then who am I *not* to at least take a chance on myself? The world would be such a better place than it already is if only more people would give themselves permission to bank on themselves.

Fast forwarding to the year 2010, I had the good fortune of traveling the world for the past 13 years as a Professional Keynote Speaker and Corporate Habits and Attitude Trainer. One day as I traveled to San Diego to speak to a group of entrepreneurs, I came across an individual who inspired me and reminded me of someone I once knew. She had a way of directing her 'fear' into 'power!' She captivated me in the way she spoke with such confidence and you could tell people looked up to her and followed her for leadership.

After the meeting was over, I had the pleasure of meeting this true leader. I explained to her how impressed I was with her and I could tell she is destined to change so many lives around the world. She leaned in to me and whispered, "please follow me, I have a secret and I don't want the others to hear." So, I followed her around the corner away from the others. She looked to the left, then to the right, then squared me off and said, "I was so scared up there on stage and I was afraid people could see right through me and my fear. Do you think anyone noticed that I was shaking up there?"

I was so surprised to hear this as I saw the complete opposite in her. Isn't it amazing how sometimes it takes the outside world to take a peek inside of you to share with you how truly powerful we truly are? I promptly explained to her that not only did we not notice any sense of fear in her, but we were so inspired that we all wanted to take action right away in our own journeys. "That's what a true leader does," I explained. I went on to suggest to her that she may want to listen to her own teachings as she clearly moved others to action, isn't it time for her to move herself to action and become that *Fearless Entrepreneur* that the world needs right now?

Clearly I've been speaking about our amazing Lynda Sunshine West! Lynda has a unique way of being so present with people and finding the true brilliance that lies inside of us. She has a way of looking deep under the surface to extract the goodness in each of us. She seeks out our true attributes and allows for each person she comes across to finally see the ability to grow out of our comfort zone and out from underneath our self-imposed masks in which we shield ourselves from the world. I can't think of anyone better to lead a team of *Fearless Entrepreneurs* than your fearless leader in Lynda Sunshine West!

There are certain individuals you will meet who will have a profound outlook in your life. For me it was when I met Brian Tracy and started working for him as a Senior Trainer as he became my first mentor in my lifelong career and journey in the self-development space. For you, my suggestion is to allow Lynda Sunshine West be *your* mentor to the fearless entrepreneurship journey you are embarking on with fantastic generational growth.

My motto has always been and I suggest you adopt it and grow from it as well: "NDSO!" No Drama - Serve Others!

To your Awesomeness & Success,

Erik "Mr. Awesome" Swanson

10 Time #1 Best-Selling Author, Professional Keynote Speaker, CEO/Founder of Habitude Warrior International & Habitude Warrior Masterminds
Author of *Crush & Dominate - 13 Strategies to Piss Off Your Competitors, 13 Steps to Riches* and *Secret Habitude Warriors*

www.SpeakerErikSwanson.com

A Sunny Note from Lynda

Welcome to *The Fearless Entrepreneurs*!
Since you've picked up this book, chances are you are an entrepreneur who is stuck while facing a daunting challenge (or two or five). Or maybe you are someone who just needs a pep talk to help get you through a difficult time.

We all need a boost every now and then to help us climb our personal mountains. There is no shame whatsoever in asking for help from an expert. The only shame, perhaps, is not receiving such a gift with gratitude when it is placed before us—whether we are able to follow the advice or not.

I've been blessed by connecting with amazing entrepreneurial souls who are making a positive impact on the planet by throwing caution to the wind and doing what they love. They are living their purpose and are loving every minute of it. If you're in a space where you're struggling with your business and aren't sure where to turn, I have your back—as do all of the wonderful contributors to this book. Know that there is a solution to every problem and someone knowledgeable in your circle of contacts is ready, willing, and able to help you. All you need to do is *ask*!

If you do happen to stumble backwards—as I have on more occasions than I care to admit—you must get right back up on your feet and learn from your experience. You will be amazed at how failure often leads to even greater opportunity and success down the road.

Why *The Fearless Entrepreneurs*?

If you think about it, every single thing on the planet (that is not indigenous) was made by an entrepreneur. Entrepreneurs are those crazy people you are saying, "You gotta have work/life balance" to because they are so passionate about what they do and the impact they're making. They are driven and, therefore, often seen as crazy.

If this is you, then you know what I'm talking about. Well, you're in the right place because these authors are just like you.

My goal—which is shared among all of the contributors to this book—is to add all of our collective advice to help you grow your business. We want to see you accomplish all of your dreams and goals and flourish.

What Is This Book About?

One morning I woke up and, before my feet hit the floor, God sent me a message saying, "You're going to write collaboration books with entrepreneurs to share their story. Their story has power and YOU are the one to get their message into the public." I heeded the word and stepped right into it.

The first book was titled *Momentum: 13 Lessons From Action Takers Who Changed the World*. Next, two titles came: *The Fearless Entrepreneurs* and *Invisible No More; Invincible Forever More*. And, so, just like any other entrepreneurial endeavor, the journey began.

The main intent of this book is to spotlight the content of the contributors in a way that is accessible, actionable, and, hopefully, entertaining.

I would characterize this book as a business (non-religious) compilation of journeys from entrepreneurs who have made the leap to create the life they truly want to live. The mission is to provide lessons that are intended to help you address and problem-solve issues related to your business.

The backgrounds and accomplishments of the contributors are all true. Their observations, principles, and lessons are 100% authentic to their business practices and philosophies. All of these brilliant individuals were an integral part of developing the content for this book. *The Fearless Entrepreneurs* would not have been possible without them. Please feel free to contact them via their websites—they would love to hear from you!

A Special Note About the Charity

100% of the net proceeds of the sales of this book will be donated to Lemonade Day, a 501(c)(3) nonprofit charity whose mission is to help prepare youth for life through fun, proactive, and experiential programs infused with life skills, character education, and entrepreneurship. For further information or to make a donation, visit their website at www.lemonadeday.org.

CHAPTER ONE

~

The Fearless Entrepreneurial Mindset Is All That You Need

by Dennis Haber
President, Haber Consulting Group, Inc
www.DennisHaber.com

This book will show you how to excel at being a FEARLESS ENTREPRENEUR. It will help you shine at the game of BUSINESS MUSICAL CHAIRS. In business, it's not about who wins and who loses. It's really about who is able to STAY IN THE GAME. It is the difference between short-term thinking and long-term thinking. Long-term thinking is manifested by leaving your employees, staff and business in better shape than they would ordinarily be. The goal is to ensure that you and your business SURVIVE and then THRIVE. You never want to become that dreaded business statistic: HAVING FAILED SOON AFTER LAUNCHING.

There are 3 COGNITIVE principles that must be front and center BEFORE you can go into business. Do not start a business unless and until you become self-aware of the ideas noted below:

KEY THOUGHT #1: As a fearless entrepreneur, you must be able to lead yourself and others. Leadership begins with a thought. Thoughts are things that influence other things. Instead of letting thoughts rattle around in your head, capture the important ones noted in this chapter.

KEY THOUGHT #2: Look at things as they are and figure out how to make changes to the work and business environment as you would like them to be. Determine what it would take to realize the desired adjustments, then make them. If you don't have this ability yet, then acquire the capacity and capability to make them. Never fight against nor fail to recognize what already exists.

KEY THOUGHT #3: It's always challenging and difficult to PREDICT the future. Stop doing it. CREATE THE FUTURE instead. It's much more predictable.

The 3 KEY THOUGHTS above and the BUSINESS WISDOM contained below will provide you with the seeds for nurturing and hatching your entrepreneurial plans. To enjoy new levels of business success, you have to internalize, accept and follow the guidelines percolating in this book. When you ignore these salient points, any success you have may be entirely due to luck and chance. At some point, the uncertain future will likely catch up with you. This will happen when you are neither prepared nor aware.

You never, for example, want to be the turkey before Thanksgiving. They feel safest (the turkeys are nurtured and well fed) when they are most at risk. As a *Fearless Entrepreneur*, you can never be complacent. Success is never final. Successes often cause management to miss signs that something is actually awry. And just like our turkey, when you feel the safest, you are not. You won't even know that catastrophe is lurking around the corner. Kodak ignored digital photography. Blockbuster ignored Netflix. What are you ignoring?

As a *Fearless Entrepreneur*, you must be aware of certain fundamentals. Just as a house will crumble and fall without a strong foundation, your business will do the same. Your competition wants you to remain unaware. Your competitors hope you never gain the significant wisdom noted herein. This book will make your competitors very nervous.

BUSINESS WISDOM-The Work Environment

The type of work environment you create determines how decisions are made, how information flows, and how power is wielded. There is a big difference between a leader and a boss.

No one questions a boss. Information is often retained by *the privileged few*. Obedience and conformity are rewarded. Workers and staff are mere followers. You do what you are told to do. When you don't follow, severe consequences are not far behind. Blind obedience to autocratic bosses no longer works. A boss is not a leader. A leader is never a boss.

A leader shares a vision with all who work for the company. Rules are not important. Instead, **values** rule the day. Information is shared with all. The liberating feeling of trust freely flows between people and groups of people, as relationships prosper. When these things happen, real communication ensues, and creativity leads to sounder solutions.

A boss asks, "How do I compel my workers to give me what I want?"

A leader asks, "How do I create a phenomenal work environment where everyone can flourish, and even get to reuse some of their learned new skills outside of work?"

Unlike a boss, a leader is always asking another fundamental question: *How would the person I hope to be do the thing I'm about to do?*

Leaders also look toward the future by working backwards. In order for your customers and clients to realize that your company should be their **go to** *company*, your employees must act in accordance with the company's vision and mission.

This is clearly manifested when the default mindset coalesces around the idea THIS IS HOW WE DO BUSINESS HERE. You hit the mark when your customers and/or clients say things like: *They make me feel important; they get it right each time; we get great value.*

This, of course, is the end result of great leadership.

BUSINESS WISDOM-The Right Metrics

Only that which is measured can be controlled. Metrics let you know what is working and what is not working.

If you measure everything, you are measuring nothing. There is no reason to do carpet bombing when a surgical strike will suffice. Deciding what measurements will provide you with intelligent feedback is crucial to survival and growth.

Following a desired set of metrics constantly forces you to re-evaluate your capabilities, the processes you employ and the priorities you give to each. Since marketing, sales, administration and operations are components in every business, you may want to track such things as: Weekly revenues, receivables and payables; amount of customer engagements; sales commitments; cashflows; production and service capacity; customer retention, etc.

When a problem arises, you must make certain that you are defining the problem and not a symptom that may be mistaken for the problem. By analyzing the data points you are tracking, you can adjust and re-adjust goals and processes as you put needed improvements in place.

BUSINESS WISDOM-The Vision & The Mission

In order to get the right employees doing the right job, the company vision must be clear so a culture can form. It is urgent that you distill this to EVERYONE in the company so they can activate the company mission.

Think of a couple of uber successful people whom you admire and whose traits you would like to showcase. Here, for example, are a few qualities you may wish your employees and staff to follow: Does the right thing; collaborate; prideful; teamwork is front and center; asking questions is more important than telling; NO SUBSTITUTE for honesty; and evidences a burning desire to be better. This is by no means an all-inclusive list.

Your biggest mistake will be to assume that each person shares your vision and is ready to acknowledge them in the everyday mission of the company. In order to reach the level of success you desire, you need to make sure that everyone is *rowing in the same direction at the desired speed. Business forces* are at work to make YOUR company irrelevant. Only constant improvement, incessant innovation, and internalization of the vision will let you remain in the game.

Another big mistake management makes is to assume because things are *going well,* investment in customer and "office" relationships can now be ignored. When people feel discarded and unheard, the work and business environment can quickly turn toxic. Relationships MUST ALWAYS be nurtured.

As an owner, you want to help your staff and employees develop the skill to grow new skills. When the staff is challenged to be better and to do more, they can quickly develop the capability to solve problems and to see issues before they develop into big problems. Problem solving abilities stems from experiencing various situations. Businesses that merely tell employees and staff what to do never accomplish nearly as much as those who permit employees and staff to learn from actual experiences.

A company can have only one standard of dependability. This concept applies within and without the company (independent contractors and suppliers). Here's an important question to ask yourself: Will my employees, customers and suppliers agree with my avowed standard of dependability? This idea, expressed in different ways, mirrors this same zeitgeist: *You can count on us....always. My word is our bond* and *If I said we'll do it; it will be done every time.* When everyone in the company can freely and honestly express these types of *dependability thoughts*, you have done a wonderful job as a leader.

It's time to become a *fearless entrepreneur*. Even though this journey is a challenging one, you can start creating a future filled with pride, hope and accomplishment. As you proceed down this exciting path, make these seminal principles follow you like a shadow. When you think differently, you can leap into your dreams, and live that magical life.

Remember, your thoughts and actions affect how long you remain in the difficult and treacherous game of Business Musical Chairs. Your leadership skills will determine not only whether you survive, but whether you thrive. It's all up to you. That is what you want, isn't it?

As you read the chapters in this book, imagine how you can apply each author's lessons to your own business.

You ARE a Fearless Entrepreneur.

CHAPTER TWO

～

From FearFull to FearLess

by Lynda Sunshine West
Founder, Women Action Takers
www.WomenActionTakers.com

I was 5 when I ran away from home. I was gone an entire week. Where did I go? That's the first question most people ask me. But that's certainly not the most important question. What could compel an innocent little five-year-old girl to run away?

I grew up in an extremely volatile household, filled with alcohol and abuse. Fear ran rampant in my childhood. Why did I run away? I decided in my pure innocent wisdom that I was not going to live in that house anymore. With those people. So I ran away to the safety of the neighbor's house. It made no difference that it was only two houses away. For all intents and purposes, it was a world away from my house. And I was planning to be gone forever. I never wanted to go back.

After a week, my mom brought me home. And what happened at my return is something that would shape the way I lived my life for decades to come. I came home with my tail between my legs and my head hung low. I refused to look anyone in the eye for many years.

I was riddled with fear.

Fear, in all of its millions of varieties, had stopped me from doing so many things I dreamed of, including running my own business. I felt paralyzed when trying to take action. I was haunted by the risk of failing so much so that I would not even try. I just could not stomach "returning home" a failure like when I was 5.

I know that I am not alone in this battle against fear of failure. It is one of the top fears most people have. However, perhaps the greatest fear that the majority of people fight against is actually the fear of judgment.

Fast-forward in time to age 51. This is where my "fearless entrepreneur" story begins.

I started working when I was 16 with your typical fast food minimum wage job at Carl's Jr. Over the next 36 years, I worked in 49 different corporate positions! Can anyone top that? Yet, I was never fired. I would get bored, feel under-appreciated, and would just move on to something new. Forty-nine times! I guess you can say I wasn't afraid of change!

As I look back on my work career, I realize my job hopping was a dysfunctional pattern that started when I was that 5-year-old little girl. I could just move on when things were not to my liking. I clearly remember one particular day when I was driving to job #49. I was a Legal Secretary to the #2 judge in the Ninth Circuit Court of Appeals. This was the penultimate job for me. I had been a legal secretary for 20 years and I had finally "made it." I began asking myself the quintessential questions. What is the purpose of this planet? What is my purpose on this planet?

My answers would come through a life coach. Hiring her is one of the best gifts I have ever given myself. Working with her helped me to discover who I really am, what value I have to offer, and who I can serve.

I wish those answers came as fast as I just typed that previous sentence! It actually took nearly six years before I could begin to completely and fully answer those questions. It has been an amazing journey and, in many ways, I am still on the journey. I am grateful to that coach for helping me make those discoveries which put me on the path to entrepreneurship. I am deeply grateful to myself for raising my hand and saying, "I deserve this. I am worthy."

On New Year's Day 2015, at the age of 51, I decided I was going to do things differently. This declaration came on the heels of an epiphany I had at the end of 2014 when I said, "I am going to quit my job and become an entrepreneur. I'm going to become a millionaire in a year." In the face of the grim statistics that most entrepreneurs fail in the first two years of business, I was determined to beat those odds. I was not about to fail at this. I had spent 36 miserable years working for other people and I knew I was not going to go back to that! I would not go back. I was determined to succeed.

Even with the profound transformations I experienced working with my life coach, I acutely recognized that fear was stopping me from living the life I wanted. Then it hit me! I decided to stop running from those fears and, instead, face them head-on. I created a personal challenge: to face a fear every single day for the entire year of 2015. The time had come for me to take my power back.

It went something like this . . . the first thing I would do every morning was to ask myself, "What scares me?" Then I stayed in bed waiting for the answer to come. The FIRST fear that came into my mind was the fear I "committed" to breaking through that day. This wasn't a New Year's Resolution. This was a COMMITMENT to change. A COMMITMENT to myself. I asked this ONE question 365 days in a row. And it changed my life.

Being an entrepreneur is the perfect laboratory for facing 365 fears (and more)! The uncertainty of entrepreneurship is daunting, even terrifying. I used to be that person at networking events who would sit in the back corner, head buried in my phone. I was too anxious to start a conversation. And my mind would go blank if someone started a conversation with me. I was too scared to raise my hand and offer a comment or ask a question. I felt paralyzed trying to use my voice. I realized these behaviors were deeply rooted in the master fear: the fear of judgment. What if I say the wrong thing? What if I sound ignorant (like my ex-husband told me on a daily basis)? What if I make a fool of myself? So many "what if's." And so I would queue up another round of solitaire on my phone.

Now as a Fearless Entrepreneur and "The Fear Buster," I help women entrepreneurs gain the confidence to charge what their services are truly worth. I also guide them to develop clarity in their message so they can attract clients to them and focus their business to get faster results. I grossly undercharged for my services for the first five years of running my business. I was trapped by the fear that my clients would not like me if I charged too much. I operated from the place that it was better to be liked than to be paid well. Now that the fear of judgment has dissipated, I stand solid in the confidence of the true value of my services and my clients love working with me.

I also used to be so unclear with my message that even my mentor didn't know what I did! He told me ever so bluntly, "Lynda, I have no idea what you do." By him saying that with such plainness, I realized I was confusing people by my message and I needed to get to clear if I wanted to attract clients to me. Confused people don't buy. Clarity is what speaks to clients.

When I became an entrepreneur, I started seven business ideas at one time! No one was going to tell me I should do just one thing. I had been a caged animal for too many years and now I was released into the wild world of entrepreneurship. For the first time in my life, I was making my own decisions and would run my business my way.

I was not having anyone tell me what to do or not to do. This was my right of freedom! And it had consequences. My lack of focus resulted in tremendous expenditures of both time and money for me to truly understand the necessity of "focus." In hindsight, I highly recommend entrepreneurs follow one venture until it becomes successful. And then when that business is running successfully on its own, start another.

I also learned that if the first course is not successful, drop it and move on. How do you know when it's time to drop it and move on? You listen to your body and feel it in your gut. Learn to feel the difference between the feeling of fear and the feeling of misalignment. And how do you know the difference? Ask yourself this question out loud: "What am I scared of?" If the answer is "nothing," then you know it is not fear making the decision to quit, but that it is simply time to drop the project and move on. Now, I can hear what you are thinking! And don't worry! This doesn't mean you are a "quitter." It means you are astute in evaluating your situation and making a decision to redirect your efforts and resources when necessary. It is actually brilliant! (Again, as long as it is not fear that is stopping you.) Do not waste time and money trying to fit a square peg into a round hole. But then again, I am not one to tell you how to run your business. You're the boss!

The abusive environment of my childhood kept a stranglehold on me. No matter what I did well, my traumas kept overpowering me. I continued to believe I was stupid and plain ignorant. I know some people who grew up in a similar environment and they are able to use the abuse to fuel them to do better. That wasn't my story, though. I felt shriveled up and small and so disbelieving in myself. I chose that story until I went through my personal transformation and self re-discovery. Remember how strong and brave I was at five years old?! I was becoming that take-charge little girl again. I decided on a new storyline for the life ahead of me: I was now accepting full responsibility for my actions and for my life. I was done blaming my childhood for the decisions I was making today. This included the abuse, the alcohol, my mom, my dad. I was done blaming them for everything amiss in my life today.

I read in Jack Canfield's book, "The Success Principles," that the first principle of success is to take 100% responsibility for your life and actions. That hit me hard. It was actually my wake-up call that I had been making a lot of excuses as to why I wasn't living the life I desired. Blaming others is the exact antithesis for taking responsibility for one's self. Once I started accepting responsibility for my own actions, doors opened and my life changed even more. Facing a fear everyday was simply the tool I chose to use in order to step into my new life, my brilliance, my confidence, my growth, and my self. My True Self.

On a random morning, the answer to my daily question, "What scares me?" was extremely specific: approach and talk to a stranger in Starbucks. I had used Starbucks as a remote office like many entrepreneurs. I would immediately pull out my laptop, start working, and definitely not make eye contact with anyone. While it may seems like a small, even silly, fear, it was actually a crippling fear for me. Fear is fear. My decision to face a fear every day for a year was a commitment to myself for growth. And, boy, how I grew!

Back at Starbucks, I was standing in a corner, watching people come in, place their order, and leave with their coffee. One man came in, placed his order, and then he sat down. My victim! My target was a person sitting alone so I could have a conversation with them. And there he was: alone, sitting, waiting for his coffee. I was finally going to face this fear. I stood there, staring at him, desperately trying to come up with my opening line of the conversation.

After he picked up his coffee and returned to his table, I slowly walked over to him, knees trembling, throat locked up, palms and forehead sweaty, stomach all knotted up. Praying my voice would not fail me, I managed to say, "Hi, sir. I'm facing a fear every day this year. And today's fear is to talk to a stranger in Starbucks." He responded suspiciously good-humored, "Okay!?"

So far, so good. I got the words out of my mouth in a coherent manner and he responded.

"Do you mind if I have a seat?"

"Sure. Please have a seat."

I chatted with him for about five minutes, stood up and said, "Thank you for your time. You helped me break through this fear. I appreciate it." I turned and walked out of Starbucks. I felt like throwing up. But I didn't.

I believe we are all born with brilliance inside of us. While it seems like it took a while to tap into it, I feel it was necessary the way it unfolded so I would have compassion for those going through what I went through. I get it now. My journey is my journey. I wouldn't change it for the world. It has been an amazing ride . . . and it ain't over yet! I am fired up about the future, even though I have no idea just how amazingly it will all unfold. I have stopped running away. Now I run toward the future. I have stopped being ruled by fear. Now I am empowered and inspired by the smallest inkling of fear. I take actions BECAUSE I'm scared. Go ahead and judge me for that!

CHAPTER THREE

~

Even a Stroke Won't Stop Me

by Alice Pallum
Founder/CEO, AMP Enterprises, LTD
www.AMPBusinessCoaching.com

I t's incredibly difficult knowing something is wrong with you and not being able to put a finger on what it is, much less how to fix it. Don't get me wrong, I'm used to fixing problems, but this was a whole different challenge. Let's start at the beginning.

In February of 2014, I incorporated by company—AMP Enterprises, LTD. After spending 17 years in corporate America and having my job eliminated—I was ready to be in charge of my own destiny.

The foundation I had built at IDS and then American Express Financial Advisors and then finally at American Express, gave me a launching pad. I had spent those 17 years solving problems. Everything from training and supporting Financial Advisors and their use of technology to delivering that technology.

When you run a department in companies that size—in my case, Field Technology—it is like running a company. You have all the same responsibilities—Goal Setting, Planning, Accountability, Performance Management, Profit & Loss, etc. As I said, a great foundation.

I really enjoyed and found it very satisfying to now help small business owners overcome obstacles and succeed.

Fast Forward to 2012—one morning in August—I woke up with a terrible headache and double vision. The headache wasn't so much of an issue, but the double vision was another matter entirely. After several hours, it had not gotten any better. I called one of my best friends, Jim, and shared what was happening. He said, "I'll be right there." He took me to the clinic—who in turn sent me off to the hospital. They were expecting us and showed me right to a bed in the ER. While there, I was waiting and wondering how long this would take. I had things to do! One of which was to visit my Mom. I let my brother know I was getting checked out at the hospital as the double vision was not going away. And this is where my memory stops. Apparently, I called my brother again to let him know that I was being moved by ambulance to a different hospital. I don't remember that call or the ambulance ride or the next 10 days in intensive care. My family was very supportive and filled in the gaps. It appeared I had had 2 strokes. The first had happened overnight and caused the headache and double vision. The second actually happened at the hospital and caused all the rest of the fun! This gets us back to that feeling of knowing something is wrong, but you don't know how to fix it. I could tell I wasn't quite thinking right, but what to do about that? The next couple days in the hospital were interesting. Tests like "can you find your way back?" The staff would take me to a different part of the floor and observe me to see if I could find my way back to my room. Then it got to be from different floors. And the scary thing is that it was HARD.

The next phase was to go to a nursing home for occupational therapy. I was only 48 and in a nursing home. I had gone from helping business owners solve complex problems and processes to someone who could not even name 5 animals that started with "f." My time at the nursing home was spent working on small motor skills like writing to thinking tasks such as puzzles and crossword. I also spent time regaining my strength and beginning to learn how to live life again.

My road to recovery was challenging—I went from the one who was always helping to the one who needed help. The next challenge was where to go after the nursing home. I still had double vision and was still working on a lot of things. I could not go home—as I live away from town and alone. My brother and his family said, "of course you are coming here."

After a fun home inspection—which also included making sure I could walk up and down the stairs and run the microwave, I moved into the spare room for 9 months. I have some great memories of that time. My nephew Matthew (age 8) giving me simple math problems to, as he put it, "help Aunt Alice with her brain." I always read to the kids. Now, after my stroke it was Elizabeth (age 9) who was reading books to me because I could not see well enough to read. It was as if my life had come full circle. This was a great silver lining to spend so much quality time with them.

Once my recovery started progressing, I slowly started attending my BNI (Business Network International) chapter meetings again. Another member of the chapter picked me up and gave me a ride to the meeting and another member would drive me back to my brother's house. This was a great step as it got me started on developing my "new normal." Attending and participating in the meetings allowed me to get started putting all that I had learned in occupational therapy to practical use. Things that I had once thought were so simple like standing up and talking with other members and presenting to the group. These had been ingrained in me, but I essentially had to relearn them after the stroke. BNI members were an incredible help to me throughout my recovery. I reconnected with longtime friends and colleagues and the organization itself really supported me after the stroke. The Executive Director of BNI Minnesota and Northern Wisconsin, Nancy Giacomuzzi, provided me with the first opportunity to start working. She reached out and offered me the opportunity to help business owners find a chapter with an opening for their profession. This was done all remotely and it gave me the opportunity to start contributing. One of the leaders organized a benefit in my honor, which is something I will always remember.

With more experience at BNI meetings, I began to see more and more improvement. My brain function improved, and I started putting sentences together more fluidly, which helped with my public speaking and normal interactions with others.

As my condition continued to improve, I began conducting BNI trainings again, as I had done in the past. A friend and colleague volunteered to drive me to my appointments and these trainings. I had a very hard time accepting this help and a mutual friend sat me down one day and said, "your friend Chuck wants to help you, let him help you." So, I did. In fact, he even drove me to a neighboring state to train!

I got better at answering questions and had to relearn one of my specialties, being able to "read a room." One of the consequences of the stroke is a right-side peripheral vision cut. This also caused me to have to give up many of my lifelong hobbies—motorcycle riding, snowmobiling, drag racing, photography, and much more. In addition to relearning how to read the room, it was hard to physically see if someone had their hand up with a question during the training sessions. As time passed, I got more comfortable sharing this peripheral vision issue with attendees of the trainings. "If you are trying to get my attention, I literally might not see you." I was amazed at how welcoming people were when I shared some of my challenges.

It took almost two years to start feeling like I was thinking as I had before the stroke. It has been a long and challenging journey and it's a ride that I feel like I'll be on for the rest of my life. Even today I still see progress that helps me to realize that we are all works in progress and it's important to give ourselves and others grace knowing that we're all dealing with issues that none of us knows about.

Today, I am more energized than ever. I have spent the last several years rebuilding and have also pivoted with today's new normal and am doing most of my business virtually. I learned during my time at IDS and American Express the importance of taking time for yourself and your family. This has become even more clear now. I always incorporate this into my consulting/coaching with my clients.

When I get frustrated with the challenges I still face—like the peripheral vision cut—I look back and remind myself that the outcome could have been so much worse. I'm thankful to be here to share my experience in hopes it will help others.

As small business owners, our personal and business lives are tightly intertwined and if one suffers, the other ultimately does as well. I'm excited to see what the future holds and I'm more excited than ever to help other entrepreneurs conquer the obstacles and reach new heights within their businesses.

We all face unique challenges in our lifetime, and it is important that we not let those struggles stop us, rather that we learn from them and chart a new course in spite of them!

CHAPTER FOUR

~

Taller Trees Require Deeper Roots

by Amy Edge
CEO + Founder, Amy Edge & CO
www.AmyEdge.com

A flashing cursor. It was mocking me.

That equivocally sums up how I felt my career was going to turn out. I was going to constantly open up a Word doc, stare at a screen, and then nothing, nada, zilch. It would mock me and stare back at me as empty as I felt. When I was young, there was only one thing I wanted, to be a writer. I wasn't particularly sure what kind of writing. I wasn't even that great at it. But, that's what I dreamed of.

I let go of that dream because of the blinking cursor. It always felt heavy. I resigned myself to finding a different path. So I leaned into pieces of the writing that I did love: the research, the outlining, the preparation, the details, the compiling. And, naturally, I decided, "I'll be a teacher." I'll spare you all the details, but at some point in this process, I became a preschool teacher.

It was great. I loved the kids. But, what I loved more than anything, was the lesson planning. I could get lost in the details and preparation.

I would sit up at night and prepare 10 pages of lessons for the week. I would structure it so that all of my students thrived, my parents would understand the outcome, and so my fellow teachers could duplicate it in their own classrooms.

My kids thrived. My parents were thrilled. My administrators were amazed.

It was the planning that lit me up. The teaching and gross 3- and 4-year olds (and their helicopter parents) were just hazards of the job. Eventually, I was promoted because of my extreme (and I mean, extreme) attention to detail. This promotion, this one new step, built the framework that would soon become the precipice of entrepreneur life.

It grounded me in what my innate skills are: the management of people, processes, projects, and planning.

My path to entrepreneurship began when life happened and we moved cities away and commuting to my career was nearly impossible. I leaned into my strengths and created the business that amplified those skills and planted my feet into the market where I knew I could impact a multitude of other business owners.

Oftentimes we are so close to our genius that we don't even realize what comes naturally to us doesn't actually come naturally to everyone else.

It's this same internal conversation that everyone has, a limiting belief that causes us to question our spectacular talents and gifts. The pieces of our soul that magnify how we intend to impact others. Our genius is how we can best serve and support others, but more often than not we see our genius as a hindrance and one of the things that makes us different.

When we are young we see being different as being worse than having the plague. But, as we enter adulthood (sometimes even later), we decide to step into our power and understand this is where we can impact others.

The main conflict I encountered when I began building the business I desired was the belief that my genius was not powerful enough to create a positive ripple effect in the world. And, even worse, that I was not enough to become a leader within the businesses I craved to partner with.

I also knew that if I allowed myself to hold myself back and not push my message to the masses, nothing would happen. No action equals no action. It takes fearlessness to become an entrepreneur. You have to be fearless to step out of the norm, out of your comfort zone.

And so I did. I wasn't an overnight success. In fact, here's a public service announcement for you: there is no such thing as an overnight success.

Success is garnered by leaning into small steps. It's taking little bits of action over time. It's creating a vision that is powerful. It's navigating through tough challenges.

That's how you make progress toward your dreams. I'm over seven years into my entrepreneurship journey and choosing to be fearless is still the best decision I've ever made. Now, I work with visionary entrepreneurs as their operations director and integrator.

Visionary entrepreneurs usually have ten new ideas every week for how to grow the reach of their organization. They see solutions in most problems and are great at connecting the dots. They see the world and their business from a 50,000 foot view. There's never a shortage of expansive and creative ventures.

These business owners, probably you reading this book right now, would most likely classify yourself as a visionary. You are a true innovator, and have so many ideas, often one right after the other! Sometimes to the point of idea paralysis (like, "There are a thousand things in my brain hole right now, what action should I even be taking? Oh, wait, here's another brilliant idea," and so on...).

Visionary leaders require visionary support since they don't work necessarily in super-linear ways. This is where my support steps in. I work as their strategic partner to be largely responsible for executing the vision and plan, as well as harmonizing operations, marketing, and finance to ensure everyone is on the same page.

As their right-hand in business, I am in charge of sailing and steering the beautiful ship that the visionary entrepreneur has already built, or is in the process of building. I like to sit in the sweet spot of having the ability to provide consistency, clarity, and organization along with being highly accountable.

I'm sure you have heard that saying, "A goal without a plan is just a wish"? This is pretty much the statement that has created the trajectory for my business. Frequently I step into the operations role in a business only to realize that the business owner is aimlessly finding their way which leads to burnout and increased stress which, in turn, results in rash decisions and products/offers that are not in alignment with their long-term, three- to five-year vision.

The biggest puzzle piece that is missing for most business owners is a strategic plan of attack or, more often than not, a strategic foundation for what their business will look like down the road, next month, next quarter, next year, and so on.

There really is nothing more powerful for your business when you create and follow a strategic business plan. A goal and a vision are powerful, but having a clear plan makes your business unstoppable.

One of the biggest roadblocks that business owners face is gaining clarity in their business. Without clarity, it's like driving with a fogged-up windshield. You might make it to your destination, but the potential for a catastrophe lies in the balance. It's hard to focus when you can't see clearly what's ahead of you. The same goes for your business. An unfocused business owner is either focusing on the wrong things or they are focusing on the right things at the wrong time.

Clarity is paramount to success and something I see with all of my visionary clients. They have a massive idea and it seems like the best next step, so they want to transition all of their energy there; however, this new project *doesn't* fit into their long-term goals or even their revenue goals. This leads to increased frustration and a decrease in energy toward the tactics that WILL increase their bottom line.

So, how do we decide which projects or initiatives we move forward with when the visionary quite literally has developed 554,894 ideas in the span of two minutes? There are seven core pillars that drive growth. Once these pillars are prioritized, we list out the initiatives under each objective, again prioritize these projects, and then begin building the foundation on when we will tackle the projects. Depending on the size of your team, the number of projects your business can simultaneously work on at a time will be different.

For each potential project, we answer these questions honestly: What is important for your business right now? Are you laser-focused on getting there? Does this initiative align with the vision, mission, and values of your business? Do you have clarity in your strategy for business growth?

Based on the answers, you'll either move forward with the project or toss it in the future jar and revisit it later.

The bottom line is that when the vision is clear, the strategy is easy. And when the strategy is in place, I am able to boil their exuberant, undeniable, change-making ideas into an executable plan that the team can easily tackle. All without the visionary having to roll up their own sleeves to figure it out.

The strongest asset that a visionary leader encompasses is their ability to cast their vision. Their weaknesses and the details is why they partner with a leader who can develop their ideas. This relationship can at times be very uncomfortable. The push back is hard, to have an idea that seems like the best thing since sliced bread and then to be told, "Wait, hold on. This doesn't align with your goals or the business" is hard to hear. But, your business is my business. Your success is my success. And, we have to strive together toward growth.

Growth is necessary and almost entirely uncomfortable, but in order to grasp onto your vision and become the changemaker and thought leader visionary entrepreneurs desire to be, you need a partner that gives you the space to be fearless enough to go for it.

Taller trees require deeper roots.

CHAPTER FIVE

~

Stand Up for Your Beliefs

by Amy Lee Kaiser
Owner, Soul Healing Bodywork &
Wellness Center
www.SoulHealingBodyworkWellnessCenter.com

Have you ever felt ignored or forgotten? Have you felt like you weren't taken seriously? These happen to be my biggest pet peeves, in business and personal relationships.

What if I told you that you can change all of this with the flip of a switch? We can overcome those feelings inside of us so that when they are expressed outside of us they hold no meaning, we don't take it personally, so it doesn't affect us.

This is true. The switch that has to be flipped is inner dialogue. The story we tell ourselves every single day. That switch is not in your head; it is in your gut just above your belly button in an energy center called the solar plexus. It's the inner work that you do to bring forth your worth. Once you've done that, it won't matter if others SEE it because you will KNOW it.

I had this experience in a meeting with an obstetrics team at a local hospital. I was meeting with them to share the pelvic work I do with women. This work can help women recover after birth, help them get pregnant, and also can help with many other pelvic and abdominal issues specific to women. As you may know, (female) medicine (even in the 21st Century) is still a male-dominated industry.

When I went into the meeting as someone who is not a doctor, someone who never went to med school, they listened to me politely. All but one male doctor. He fired questions at me but didn't give me time to answer. He was cracking jokes about the pelvic work I do, asking if I can help men with erectile dysfunction. Then he continued to tap the other male doctor on the shoulder telling him he should come to see me for his erectile dysfunction issues and was laughing (as if I wasn't important - ignored, forgotten).

Finally, after being asked five or six questions, I simply asked if he was going to give me time to answer or if he just wanted to hear himself speak. You see, in this instance, I realized this man was projecting onto me how he felt inside about himself. He was new to the practice and new to the country. He was trying to assert his dominance. He had the biggest ego in the room and, therefore, learned nothing. He did not want to be questioned or even have a mind open enough to perhaps learn something that could benefit his patients. It all came down to his feelings of inadequacy and self-doubt.

I held my own and did not allow him to make me feel small because I recognized that he felt incompetent. Unfortunately, he got nothing out of the meeting. Thankfully, a female senior doctor checked him and told him he'd be a better doctor if he learned to listen.

This is just one example of many instances where I've been chided for the work I do. And I'm damn good at it, too. Had this meeting taken place even a year earlier, I would have taken it personally and undoubtedly reacted poorly (not there in the meeting, but at home while stewing over it). I would have internalized it and gotten angry at him and myself. The self-doubt would have crept in for a few days and I would have had to talk myself out of it.

Stop right now! Ask yourself, "Am I in my Ego? Am I internalizing others' projections?" OR "Am I projecting my self-doubt onto others? Am I the arrogant jerk right now?" We've all been in both roles, all of us. That's our humanness. Learn to be quiet more often and become an observer. Read the room. How do people react when you talk or run a meeting? How do you react when others talk or run a meeting?

Every time you take on someone else's projection or lower your energy to match their shitty vibe, you slow your progress and your success. Stop doing it! I encourage you to work on your chakras, specifically the first 3, Root, Sacral, and Solar Plexus. These are the areas where, energetically, your life purpose, self-worth, creativity, and security are housed. These energy centers need to be cleared for humans to function at their optimal level. Not only do you feel more energy, confidence, and mental clarity, you feel healthier physically. There are many ways to work on these chakras. I suggest trying a few and see what works best for you.

Also, see the humanness of the person projecting. It is the quickest way to realize and keep in the forefront of your mind that they are also wounded and it has nothing to do with you. Don't you think we have enough to work through without taking on the bullshit of others? They are not our responsibility or our problem. This does not mean we do not care or cannot help, but it does mean we do not internalize it and make it our own. It means we are honoring our own boundaries.

Lastly, if you're having impostor syndrome (I think most Entrepreneurs have experienced this) or self-doubt, read the reviews of your clients. Listen to what they are saying about you. Believe them when they say you're amazing or incredible. Believe when they say you changed their life or they could not have gotten through without you.

Pay attention to how many are referring others to you. See yourself the way others see you! You're probably a lot more awesome than you think!!

When you do the internal healing, you're more focused on action steps and have the confidence to act on them. This became very useful when I decided to separate from my mentor early in 2020. I decided to disassociate for both personal and professional reasons. The win is that I left when I felt called to do so, instead of justifying or making excuses so I could stay in my comfort zone.

Many of us stay with coaches and mentors for too long because we've developed a personal relationship and friendship. We are vulnerable to them and have a sense of loyalty. However, any good coach or mentor wants you to outgrow them. They will want you to level up, outgrow, and move on to make room for others who may need them. If you feel you're being kept small or you are keeping yourself small to stay, that's a big red flag to get out as fast as you can!

As we grow and learn, we shift. Because someone was a good fit for me over two years ago, doesn't mean they are a good fit for me now and vice versa. Also, as we level up, we want to be surrounded by people supporting that growth and movement in a way that resonates with us.

And that brings me to my next point! Who are you surrounding yourself with, whether personally or in your business relationships? Are your business relationships with like-minded people on the same trajectory? You want to be sure that it FEELS good in your gut. An example I give is if you are someone very much for gun control and believe no one should have a gun unless their job requires it. You walk into a collaboration meeting and find everyone else is a card-carrying member of the NRA. Do you really want to be there? This can be an extremely heated topic! Even though this is in no way related to your business, you'll find the energy won't be right for you. Maybe they know how to make you money and get you ahead, but how will you FEEL going through that process?

Who I collaborate with is crucial and I must remain in my integrity and in my vision. We need to seek advice from others, but if that person does not know and is not open to learning about energy healing, alternative, and holistic therapies, then I won't work with them. For them to understand what I do and why I do it, they need to understand energy.

Networking is different. You want to talk to all types of people because you never know who they may know. But as far as collaborating or looking at a partnership, you've got to be on the same level.

So, where can changes be made for you to move forward and move on?

Are you standing in your integrity so you're able to call in the right people for you?

Are you holding on to your coach/mentor or other relationships because of fear or obligation?

Are you ready to shift and level up?

Your time is now!

CHAPTER SIX

~

The Crushing Blow That Saved My Life

by Andy Nam
Director, Foco Research LLC
www.focoacademy.com

I'm all about helping people live longer. But here's the thing: it's not just about "longer." It's about enjoying life and being healthy while you're living longer.
— Andy Nam

I met my beautiful wife Minna when we were in high school, on Valentine's day in 1988. We were actually both on dates with other people… and we had both been dumped. One of Minna's friends sent me a Valentine's day rose with a pretty raunchy poem inside, but signed Minna's name. I decided I had to find out who this "Minna" was.

My best buddy and I hacked into computer lab to find Minna's address. It's a joke between us now that I was stalking Minna right from the start. But when I asked her for a date, she jokingly said yes, as long as I promised to buy her a Lotus one day. "Cool," I said, and we have been together from then on.

I graduated from high school at 18 and started working full-time, so I was able to get a pretty cool little sportscar (with a little help from my dad). Every weekend, I went to Minna's house to see her.

One day in June of 1988, I was on my way to pick her up. I went through a traffic light and was broadsided on the driver's side by a one-ton U-Haul truck that ran the red light. This was made worse by the fact that he was going downhill and way too fast. He hit me, pinned my car to a telephone pole, and totaled both my car and me.

My car was smashed into a V-shape around the pole. The driver's side was completely gone. The driver's seat was in the passenger seat.

This accident fractured my neck, bent my back, dislocated my knees, and severed a part of my ear. It took me about six months to rehab. My doctor told me, "You're lucky to be alive considering the type of accident that happened to you. But, unfortunately, it's going to speed up the degeneration process. You will probably have a 70-year-old body by the time you're in your thirties." Remember, I was only 18 and in my prime, and I just ignored his warning.

Fast forward to my second year of college. I dropped out. I just could not see the value in being there. I was great with cars, so I started my own garage specializing in making cars go faster and look better, sorta like a *Fast and Furious* thing before *Fast and Furious* was a thing.

The bad thing was that, as a mechanic, I was working twelve-to-sixteen-hour days and always under or bent over a car. The pain I suffered grew steadily worse. Every day, I was taking prescription Tylenol (you know, the kind with codeine in it) to kill the pain, and later graduated to Vicodin just to get through a day.

Every morning, I had to roll out of bed, pick myself up off the floor, and go take a hot shower before I could even begin to move well enough to start my day.

I didn't realize that all that kind of work was contributing to the degeneration of my already damaged and degenerating body. I also didn't understand that taking that much medication was really messing up my entire digestive system.

My health was at serious risk.

It was a real wakeup call when my body started breaking down. I simply did not want to go that route. So I started to supplement. I tried all the different supplements out there that promised improvement, but still I suffered from the degeneration.

Minna and I married in 1999, and in 2000 I sold that garage and we moved to California. When I was 35, we bought a Lotus so I could fulfill my teenage high school promise to Minna.

But this car was small and low to the ground. My back and knees immediately felt the strain of getting in and out, not to mention sitting in one position while driving. I could drop into the car, but I couldn't get out. I would take Minna out to a nice dinner. I'd drive up in this beautiful car with my beautiful wife, but crawl out of the car like a decrepit old man.

It was humiliating.

And insanely painful.

Over the years, both Minna and I had watched family members suffer and die from chronic, degenerative diseases. I saw how those kinds of diseases affect the loved ones and holds, them hostage to a dreary lifestyle. A lot of people believe that when you suffer, you suffer alone. That is so NOT true. Everyone close to you suffers as well. My dad had Parkinson's for fifteen years before he died. I watched him waste away and I also saw my mom waste away. It was terrible. It was something that I believe no one should ever have to endure.

The turning point for me came at age 43. We were doing pretty well financially, but we had no quality of life. We couldn't travel because I could not sit or stand for more than a few minutes. Driving anywhere in the car was an ordeal. I suffered from IBS, so I couldn't eat anything, especially fine foods. I know now I was seriously depressed because I literally felt sick and tired all the time. I never smiled. One day I looked at Minna and realized how my lack of physical and emotional health was affecting her. I suddenly understood that, if something didn't change, I would lose her.

Then a miracle happened. We owned that little Lotus for eight years, and only put 12,000 miles on it. In 2013, I sold it to this young Vietnamese kid who could not have been more than 25 years old. He fell in love with the car when we took it out for a test drive. I asked him, "I'm curious. How is it that you can afford this car at your age?"

He looked at me and said, "Well, I sell drugs."

Oh sh**, I thought. I'm gonna get carjacked.

Then he started smiling at me. "Just kidding. I sell supplements."

Wait. "You sell vitamins, and you're buying a $30,000 car?" I asked, my interest piqued. None of the supplements I was taking had really done anything for me.

He told me all about a company called Usana – the whole spiel about how great it was, just everything. He bought my car, with cash, and said, "Listen, how about you just check out these vitamins."

He told me about the different vitamins and said, "This joint supplement and the Super Vitamin C are going to change your life. They work on a cellular level." He said they have a 30-day unconditional guarantee. I could try them for a month and get all my money back if I was dissatisfied.

I decided to try them all. I purchased one of each thing they had, believing I would return them in a couple weeks.

What happened next shocked me down to my core.

Two weeks into taking these Usana supplements, I wasn't taking Vicodin anymore.

At three weeks, I was walking like a normal person again. I said to Minna, "Something isn't right." It had been so long since I felt good that I had forgotten that *feeling good is supposed to be normal.*

I learned that, when your body has the right things, it will repair itself, and fast. I dove into learning about functional nutrition, and also became a fitness coach, because I wanted to learn how everything worked together.

This started me on the path to living at optimal health. We visited the Usana plant and discovered that these are literally the purest vitamins out there. This company is the only one Olympic and professional athletes can use because they can trust that they won't get a false positive on any random drug tests.

I was 43 years old when I began this journey to optimal health. Minna and I look at our health now, in our fifties. We are both healthier now than we were in our thirties, and I am far healthier than I was even in my twenties.

How many people can say that?

Now I'm all about helping people live longer. But here's the thing: it's not just about "longer." It's about enjoying life and being healthy while you're living longer. There's a big difference between living to 100, but confined to a bed at age 60, and living to 100 and still running around with everyone else, having a life.

That's my vision – to inspire others to *enjoy life* longer. I really believe that age is just a number. It's not something that's going to limit what your body can do.

I'm living proof.

> *It is health that is the real wealth and not pieces of gold and silver.*
> **— Mahatma Gandhi**

~

CHAPTER SEVEN

Ascension: Beyond Meditation

by Bhakti Ishaya
Ascension; Beyond Meditation
www.TheBrightPath.com

I'm learning what I need to unlearn.
— Bhakti Ishaya

A s a young man, I was lost. I didn't know what to do. I found myself divorced twice by age 28, a son I couldn't support and fired from every job I ever had. I was a wreck. My transition to civilian life from being in combat in Viet Nam, like many, was horrible.

I was lying in bed one night, sleepless and begging for help. I screamed out, "What am I to do?" What came through, clear as a bell, was, "Seek and follow Divine Guidance. Learn what you need to learn to become the most proficient at doing that, and also unlearn what you need to unlearn to be most proficient at doing that."

Where do I start? I wondered.

That Sunday, I went to church, which was not normally my Sunday morning routine at that time. There I heard Jesus' message, "The Kingdom of Heaven is at hand."

Hey, I thought, *"is" is a present-tense word*. It is Now. It is being present in the Presence.

Then I heard, "The Kingdom is within. Seek first the Kingdom of Heaven and all will be given."

Well, since I had nothing, I figured this was a pretty good idea. But how to do that?

The question was answered, and I learned to meditate within 30–60 days. They said to do it once a day, but because of my situation, I decided to commit and do it twice a day. I immediately began to realize the enormous benefits of letting go of my old thinking patterns.

In other words, I was learning what I needed to unlearn.

And believe me, from the way my life had been going, I needed the benefits that came from that unlearning.

Things changed; life was different.

Fast forward fifteen years. I was president and CEO of a company based in Minnesota, and my avocation had become studying meditation. But when I was brutally honest with myself, **I just knew there had to be more**. I then experienced two years of synchronicities that led me to meeting a modern-day Ishaya monk that taught the practice of Ascension.

He told me that I didn't need to believe in this practice for it to work. He explained that I could use the practice with my eyes open or closed and experience **Eternal Peace** no matter where I was or when.

My mind was chattering quite a bit when he said that. *But what if? What if he was right?*

Then I remembered the directive, "Learn what you need to learn to be the most proficient at doing that."

I found he was right. Ascension is an effective practice, of which there are very few. It allows us to circumvent the mind's chatter and experience the still, silent place within.

Ascension is basically a means to achieve the goal of what it means to be fully alive on planet Earth. In western Judeo-Christian culture, it's referred to as "the peace that surpasses all understanding," "praying without ceasing," and "oneness with God."

In the east, there are many different words, but they all point toward Enlightenment. In order to fully understand Enlightenment, you take a look at its opposite, which is ignorance. Ignorance is ignoring something that already exists. Because we are born human, we are already enlightened. All we need to do is dissolve the barriers that keep us from recognizing that. And Ascension does that.

Ascension dissolves stresses of life so that we are able to experience more and more of who we truly are in each moment. Many people have heard the phrase, "We're in this world, but not of this world." The "in this world" part means that we deal with the limited mind. We listen to what the mind is telling us. We respond via our belief systems, which is really the ego-mind directing us. We suffer the stresses of everyday life all the time. When we Ascend, we bypass all that ego-construct, and healing occurs, stress is dissolved.

That's as simple as it is.

Living life from that space, we need do nothing. All we have to do is return to who we truly are.

We refer to the still, silent place within as the Ascendent, because that word can't offend anybody. The practice is designed for everybody, globally, in all cultures. Ascension has no belief system or dogma, and therefore does not interfere with one's religious or spiritual practice.

The Ascendent is referred to in all religions by different names. In Christianity, it's also known as the Holy Spirit or the Risen Christ.

However, that is just a name. Like Shakespeare wrote, "A rose by any other name would smell as sweet."

The still, silent place within is the source of our reality. It IS all reality. After all, which cell in your body is not God? (Or Higher Power, or whatever name you choose to use. An apple is an apple in every language.)

Stress in our lives stems from when we're young. For instance, I had three older, adopted sisters. When I was three or four years old, they told me and my younger brother, "Well, we were chosen. Mom and Dad just got stuck with you." These kinds of things create a lasting imprint on a person's psyche.

Even if we grow up in perfect, loving families, we still go to school. We experience judgments and comparisons and all kinds of conflict. And then comes the hormonal turmoil of puberty. By the time we are adults, our ego-mind has created this "individual" that is supposed to be an adult and know what to do.

Since the 1970s there have been a number of peer-reviewed studies that show the positive effects of an effective daily practice. There are four basic conclusions:

- **Increased Happiness**: I am a Viet Nam veteran and suffered stress around loud noises and bright flashing lights. Even though I had meditated 20 years with other practices, that anxiety still occurred during thunderstorms. With my Ascension practice, things changed. Life was different.

- **Improved Health**: For the 5 years before I learned the practice of Ascension, I had passed a kidney stone once or twice a year. NOT a good experience. I have not passed one since.

- **Enhanced Relationships**: Rosemary and I always had a great marriage. After we learned to Ascend, our life just became pure bliss!

- **Optimal Performance**: Ascension can be the impetus for success in business. Lois Koffi, who I taught, wrote, "I did so well the first 6 months after I learned to Ascend that the company I was with bought me a new Mercedes."

The 20th Century French philosopher, scientist, and theologian Pierre de Chardin said, "We are a spiritual being having a human experience." But if he were to change one word in that statement, everything changes. Instead of saying, we are a spiritual being, he could have said we are *The* Spiritual Being having a human experience. This would mean we are not separate from the underlying Source of all Reality.

But how do we experience that? We simply look within; because inside of each one of us is a still silent open space that goes forever. It is a place where time and space have no relevance and no existence, a place where fear has no meaning, a place eternal and alive, and a place so real and accessible that all we have to do is recognize it.

It's my experience and part of the human condition that whatever we focus on manifests itself in all areas of our lives. We simply let go of all the mental constructs of the mind and take that 18-inch journey from our heads to our hearts. Then we experience Heaven on Earth within. We keep doing that, and The Divine manifests in all areas of our lives. Do that, pay attention, and be alert, and that allows you to be truly alive on this planet. From that, everything happens. Pay attention to just this moment. Because this moment is the only one that can possibly exist.

Heaven on earth is not a dream, but a quest, a destiny, and the purpose of our existence. It is our birthright. By retraining our attention to go inward and rediscovering the source, which resides within all of us, we fulfill our collective potential. And Ascension does that.

*I hesitate to call it meditation, for it is **far beyond anything I've ever experienced**. The method is incredibly simple and profoundly effective! Meditation has never been so easy.*
— LB, USA, Church Minister

CHAPTER EIGHT

~

Creating The Success Finder

by Brandon Straza
CEO, The Success Finder
www.TheSuccessFinder.com

I feel that the word "Entrepreneur" can be a loosely used term. No, I'm not here to discourage you. In fact, I want you to succeed. I feel that in today's world, entrepreneurs need an unfair advantage. Over these pages, I want to condense what took me more than twenty years to understand in the hopes that it might make you feel supported, understood, and hopeful. We've all heard people introduce themselves as an entrepreneur, and probably asked ourselves, "What does that really mean?"

When you're done reading this chapter, I want you to walk away and say:

1. I'm going to design the life I want.
2. These are the next steps I'm going to take.
3. Eventually, I'll work **on** my business as opposed to **in** my business.

4. Money will be a biproduct of what I will build; solving a problem is my goal.
5. I can step away from my business and it will still run.

It's interesting what will happen as you make these decisions. To the people currently around you, you'll end up being an outlier. You're going to leave the "wolfpack" and do things differently. You will hear the sentences:

"I want my Brandon back."

"What happened to you?"

"You never make time for me anymore."

"I don't understand what you're doing."

"We don't have the same relationship as we used to."

I've heard each of these phrases. More than once. From people I care about deeply. And at first, I didn't know how to process them or how to place them in my mental hierarchy. My human mindset hadn't yet adopted the key to my launching off point; the pivotal moment when I:

Hired a Coach. Joined the RIGHT Mastermind. And surrounded myself with the right people.

That's it. And that's everything. The whole story. Once I found my coach, and my direction, and my people, I was ready to rise up. I went on to build a seven-figure company, left a job that no longer served my purpose, and found the work I was most passionate about. I became an entrepreneur.

My one and only regret? That I didn't do it sooner.

Let the NO Drive YOU

My first business (if I'd call it that) was slinging sugar mixed with Kool-Aid® packets to the neighborhood kids. Sure, I made a few bucks, but didn't foresee that the parents of my friends wouldn't be too happy. The good news it only lasted during my first few summers and kids loved to go against their parents. The bad news, I really didn't have a sustainable model, let alone the fact that these kids could go to their own pantry and get the same product. What it did teach me was that you aren't going to make everyone happy and that was more than enough for my first business lesson.

My next model of business was looking to the man I called Dad. I had a great childhood that shaped my future self. I saw that working a traditional "9-5 job" wasn't an option. I thought that working more hours equaled success. All of this eventually turned into bankruptcy, our family name being drug through the newspaper (pre-social media days), living in poor conditions, and kids making fun of me at school because of what they heard from their parents around the breakfast table. This moment was what I'd like to call my first real NO. Though no one actually used the word NO, it was a driving force that would sit in the back of my mind to be released much later.

My next NO came from my high school algebra teacher. She explained that I didn't have what it took compared to my brother who was the salutatorian and my sister who was a world class athlete. The problem was, she never asked what I really wanted. I didn't want my brother's achievements or my sister's accomplishments. I wanted to make my own way.

Now comes the hardest NO of them all. I was getting ready to get married, I had a 6-figure job, and I wanted to break out on my own. I didn't have a problem with authority, but I wanted to be responsible for my successes and failures. I knew that relying upon someone else's company culture and ideas forced me to rely upon their decisions, good or bad. Though everyone around me said NO, "the failure rate of businesses was over 50% after 2 years," I needed the one person to stand in my corner, my wife Angela.

Building the Foundation

When I built my first company, I did a lot of business planning and strategic development. I had countless conversations. And to be honest? I made a lot of it up as I went. What I hadn't planned for was building a business where I wasn't the beginning, middle, and end. Sure, I thought that I'd eventually hire a team, but all of the steps I was creating always had to go through me. I realized this about three employees in. I was always on the phone having to answer at that point to hundreds of people.

I learned quickly that when you're the boss, you can't make it about you. Build a team that you trust and give them the confidence to make decisions on behalf of the company. Develop systems and nurture a culture that others can sustain when you're not there to run the show. If you're in sales, let your referral sources know that you have a team and that they can handle it.

Now here's a side note and it's very important: I didn't pay myself for the first 18 months. I had already hired a part-time employee and knew that if the business didn't survive, it didn't matter how much I was "paying" myself, the business would have failed. Please make sure you've run through the numbers with your spouse or business partner before making the best decision of your life. Communication today will set you up for the WIN tomorrow.

Money is the biproduct of solving the problem.
— Brandon Straza

Moving ahead, I had built my foundation but wasn't feeling fulfilled. I had left a job and created a company, built a brand, but something was missing. That was when I first heard about "Masterminds." I was intrigued and joined my first.

The process was a turning point for me, both professionally and personally.

I found out that I could learn from others in industries that had nothing to do with mine and, thus, change the trajectory of what I had already built. I learned that I am stronger when I surround myself with people who are invested in my success.

Which brings me to you today. I am invested in your success. And I want to expedite your journey.

I have just spent the last two years developing a company called "The Success Finder." I saw a great need for a community of Coaches and Members–people just like me who were looking to "Level Up" by gaining education, insight, and skills to better prepare you for professional and personal success. This isn't the place where you'll earn a 4-year degree; this is a place where you'll discover who you really are and what you really want.

Our mission is to match Coaches and Members who are ready to move workbook theories to real-world experience, to network with others, and lay the groundwork for a career path of their own design.

The Success Finder App was created to enable direct conversation between Coaches and their clients. In an era where we are all bombarded with social media notifications, friend requests, and messenger, we set out to create fast access, away from the noise and distraction. We're about providing information, immediacy and support, all housed in one personalized location.

Now this isn't a pitch for what I've built; these are the blueprints for *how* I've built. I want you to realize that being able to identify a problem, articulate a solution, arm yourself with the skills and resources you need, and surround yourself with people who are invested in your success is critical to achieving anything great. I tell everyone I meet, "you have to be willing to invest in yourself."

What does that look like for you? How can you invest today in what you hope to achieve tomorrow? You can't control the stock market, housing market, or Crypto (I'm in all of these). But you can control how well you prepare yourself to succeed. I challenge you to invest in yourself today, and to ask for help as you need it. Download The Success Finder App and message me personally.

This is my story. It's time to write your own.

CHAPTER NINE

~

Nobody Wants to Spend Their Golden Years Working at the Golden Arches

by David Smith

Founder, From Debt to Wealth to Impact

www.DavidSmithSpeaks.com

What's your lifelong dream?

I am living what has literally been the culmination of my lifelong dream. My podcast, *From Debt to Wealth to Impact*, is something that's been ruminating inside my head for as long as I can remember and it's finally out there in the public. Podcasting opens up the door for anybody to create their own stage and career and have their own platform.

This dream goes back years and years when I always thought people should move from living paycheck to paycheck (debt) through a process of being stable (wealth) to making the world a better place (impact).

It was about 10 years ago when the seed was planted into my brain. I was with a network marketing company selling weight loss products. I had this idea at the time that… Americans are worried about losing weight while there are millions of kids every day under the age of five dying from malnutrition and lack of access to medicine. Millions dying … every … day … because they can't get enough to eat while we're trying to lose weight.

I came to the conclusion that I could help more people by teaching them how to create wealth and then they can use their wealth to make an impact by giving to charities like World Vision, a Christian humanitarian organization helping children experience fullness of life, thereby impacting children, their families, and communities in need.

By helping people move from financial struggle to stability and from stability to significance, I can make the greatest impact and live my purpose to its fullest. THIS is my greatest passion and I believe that when we live our passion, we are living.

What's crazy is I've had many different business ideas and have embarked on so many journeys that I sometimes wonder why I keep going. I've been knocked down more times than I care to admit, but I keep getting up and trying something else. I have this dream, desire, and passion for entrepreneurship, and I know it's what keeps me moving forward. Even when I feel like quitting, I get back on the horse and run another race. From network marketing to reselling to online trading to cryptocurrency, you name it, I've probably done it.

As a matter of fact, I've been in and out of network marketing for what seems like FOREVER! I love network marketing because the products I've been involved with are geared toward helping people and that's my highest purpose, helping people.

I always knew instinctively that I had to sell something that I enjoyed and would make a difference for people so they would keep taking it. I never wanted to sell something just to make money. It had to make a difference first.

But that's not to say I never got involved in some stinkers. I've seen my fair share of those. I remember one in particular that was an amazing personal development company. Yes, it was a network marketing model for personal development. It sounded brilliant at the time, but they folded. I loved the idea because, again, I was going to be helping people with their personal development. When something didn't work, I would find another network marketing company to get into.

However, there came a time when I let my purpose drift aside and I chased the money.

One of the biggest turning points for me was when I was in the Extra Digit Movement. I was in the EDM training and Eric, the founder, said, "If you buy X number of copies of my book, I will throw in this webinar."

It hit me, he sells 20 copies for $197 total, that's only $9.85 each, then I can mark them up and sell them on eBay for a small profit. It was stunning. I sold all 20 of them in a weekend. I thought it was nuts and amazing at the same time. I realized I could sell on eBay to pay for my network marketing auto-ship plus my marketing costs.

Then a buddy of mine told me about a company that taught people how to sell on eBay with drop shipping. This was brilliant because it was literally what I had thought of. That was one of my major turning points. I did pretty well with that. The beauty of it was that I was selling on eBay and making money and it didn't matter if I was good at recruiting and marketing the educational side of it or not. I did fairly well building it up a little bit.

Then Roger, the owner of the training company, started teaching how to make money on Amazon, and so I went into Amazon. But I went in a different direction than what they were all about, getting a product from China and launching your own product, private labeling it. That was cost prohibitive for me, but there were other ways to sell on Amazon. Roger said, "I can teach you, and I have taught most of you, how to make money, and most of you have managed to screw it up. And it's because of what goes on up here" (he was pointing to his head). That's when he introduced us to some ideas around reprogramming our mind about how we think about money. And that was where I got latched on to it, because that's what I wanted to know.

Over the years I've sold hundreds of thousands of dollars of products on Amazon. But even that didn't come without its challenges.

It was weird because I can sell successfully on eBay and make a certain amount of money, but no higher. Why is it that I can sell on Amazon and make a certain amount of money and not go any higher? I would sell up to a certain level and then my subconscious mind would kick in and go, "You're not supposed to have that kind of money," and I would start taking wrong actions. The next inventory buy that I made would completely suck, I would lose it all and have to start over again. I probably restarted my Amazon business three different times.

I started learning about how the subconscious mind works in regards to money and every area of our life and realized that was the next step in my evolution. Learning how to reprogram my mind to basically accomplish almost anything I wanted to accomplish.

I had a fear around money. I wouldn't spend enough money on inventory to go to the next level because my fear wouldn't allow me to spend more. I felt comfortable and wanted to stay in my comfort zone. Spending $200, $300, or $400 a week on inventory was where I was stuck and it wasn't getting me where I wanted to go.

I realized my fear was stopping me, so I followed this audio program to reprogram my mind around money and comfort zones and all of the stuff. And then I made a decision that I was going to "hit a five-figure month on Amazon in the next 30 days." And I knew that for that to happen I would have to have five figures worth of inventory in the warehouse.

I still remember to this day, the first weekend. We used a method called retail arbitrage, where you go out and buy products at regular stores, whether it was on clearance or if it was just items that happened to be hot for whatever reason, because they were scarce. And then I would put them in the Amazon warehouse and Amazon would sell it and they would fill the order and do everything. We had to actually go out to retail stores on the weekends and buy inventory. And I remember it just like it was yesterday (even though that was three or four years ago).

That first weekend that we went out we spent around $1,300 and I felt like I was about to have a heart attack. That was three times more than I had ever spent in one weekend. But by this point I knew what I was doing, so, while I was a little nervous, I knew what I was doing and knew the stuff was going to sell. The idea was to sell it fast enough to get the money back and then go out and do it all over again. I spent about $4,500 on inventory in a 30-day period and, over the following 30-day period, made $11,300. Where previously my fear and my comfort level kept me down (the biggest risk I had ever taken was $500 – and that one failed), I realized I had been self-sabotaging myself.

I was still working my job at FedEx and discovered that retail arbitrage was so hard to scale. I stayed in that $11,000 to $14,000 range for a little while until I just realized that it was a grind and then decided not to push as hard.

What's interesting is $300 to $400 was my comfort zone, then moving to my next level of $4,500 became my comfort zone, then moving to $14,000 became my comfort zone and soon became a grind and too hard to keep pushing for it.

I was going to stop, but every time my friend and I went to a convention of some sort, we found ourselves going into stores looking for products. We could buy shoes and mark them up and then after about the third restock, other sellers found out about the product and the price would tank. I was so addicted to reselling, it's such a great rush, even though it's a grind. To find something for one price and sell it for a higher price? There's nothing quite like it.

Even though I loved it, I decided to get into something that isn't such an up and down market and could be sustainable: coaching and public speaking. I entered a public speaker training program and was on my way to my first speaking gig in Las Vegas when, suddenly, Vegas shut down. Covid-19 hit. As you know, the whole world ended up shutting down. Again, one of my dreams was brought to a halt.

But, as I said at the beginning of this chapter, I just keep getting up and moving forward.

I found Facebook Marketplace and took it for a spin. In my first 45 days, I went from zero to five figures. It was nuts. I was shocked at how fast I made so much money. Then the shoe dropped. The Facebook algorithm changed and I went from five figures to almost nothing in one week.

The ups and downs of entrepreneurship can really get you down at times, but if you keep your sights on your passion and keep driving forward, you will eventually get the result you're looking for. You gotta have faith in what you're doing and who you're here to serve.

Nobody wants to spend their golden years working for the golden arches. I watched my dad fall victim to not getting past this grind and working for Wal-Mart, even in his 70s. It breaks my heart. This is why I'm so passionate about helping people go From Debt to Wealth to Impact.

CHAPTER TEN

~

Sometimes You Flop; It's How You Handle the Flop That Counts

by Elizabeth Moors
Creator & Founder, Navigating Aspergers
www.ElizabethMoors.com

I didn't start out as a fearless entrepreneur. If I had, things would look a lot different today. You see, I competed in entrepreneurship in high school within the state and the country. In fact, in 12th grade, I won 1st place in California and 3rd in the country. I truly did not want to attend college. I wanted to be out on my own forging ahead. However, instead of following my passion (which at times I do regret); I followed societal norms by going to college and getting a Bachelor Degree in marketing. Although, at the time, I didn't think the degree was going to help me on my journey; in hindsight, it was very useful in acquiring skills needed to pursue my own business. It also afforded me the opportunity to hold several management positions for approximately seven years. While working, it was apparent that I wasn't made to work a 9 to 5 job, so to speak. I believe that there are some of us who are meant to work 9 to 5 and there are some of us who are meant to follow our passions and create our work. Being an entrepreneur is not an easy "job" and it's definitely not for everyone. In fact, it's the toughest "job" you'll ever have, but it's also the most rewarding—even at its most difficult times.

Before you become an entrepreneur, let alone a fearless one, we should look at the definition of an entrepreneur. An entrepreneur is considered an individual or individuals that create a new business while bearing most of the risks and enjoying most of the rewards. They are commonly seen as an innovator of new ideas, goods, services, procedures and/or business. There are several different types of entrepreneurs, I'm only going to discuss briefly three of them. If you are currently an entrepreneur, then it's a refresh; if you are considering becoming one, it's a little introduction.

Now, what is considered an entrepreneur. There are varying types of entrepreneurship. The first one is an individual who works for someone, but is considered a 1099 employee. This type of employee (although paid by a company) is paid on his/her abilities to sell a product or service. Easily put if you don't work, you don't get paid. This is a great way in my opinion to be an entrepreneur. I did this for quite some time and although you don't have 100% control of your time unless of course you don't need to make any money, you get to make an incredible income and have some control over your time. This form is also great because you are typically using the company's marketing, HR, IT department, etc. It's the best of both worlds.

Another type of entrepreneurship is as a solopreneur aka sole proprietor. With this type, you are the business. You wear all the hats related to running a business. You are every department. What's great nowadays about being a solopreneur is that you can contract with others to handle those areas of business that you either don't like or have no

THE FEARLESS ENTREPRENEURS

real experience in. The choice is yours. Your business succeeds or fails based upon your actions or inactions.

The last type is as a small business owner. Typically to be a small business owner, you need to have some employees. Just like a solopreneur, you are in charge of every aspect of your business; however, you employ others that are more experienced in the fields that you are not. Your business succeeds or fails based on your actions or inactions.

Now for all entrepreneurs, there are sometimes outside factors that you cannot control or necessarily plan for. I personally have experienced several of these. It is at this point that decisions need to be made quickly. Do you just fold? Do you regroup? Go back to the drawing board? At this juncture, you are put to the entrepreneur test.

Case in point, COVID. No business was prepared for this economic catastrophe. Numerous small businesses had to close their doors, some never came to fruition, while others scrambled to regroup and find other methods to get their product or service out to their customer and some survived by the skin of their teeth. Although this caused hardship to many, there were many opportunities discovered during this time as well. Some of those opportunities led to new industries being born and saw successful small businesses forging a new path. As an entrepreneur, you need to be able to adapt as quickly as possible. For some of us that's hard, we're not so good at change (I'm in that boat), but if we aren't willing to take that next wave, we'll be beached.

How did I become a fearless entrepreneur? Simply put, it's because I never gave up on my dream or myself. My life has literally seen its share of curve balls, interruptions and distractions. Just when I'd start gaining momentum on my journey, something would happen. I'm not talking little things, but major curve balls. Every decade of my life, I've had a serious medical issue. The last one being heart surgery, a supposed seizure, and a stroke at the ripe old age of 50, but here I am stronger than ever.

It was during this phase of my life that I came up with my million dollar idea (at least to me). It's definitely innovative and would make a difference to many of us. So, why hasn't it come to fruition? What's holding me back? Although I'm considered fearless by many, we all have moments of wondering if this "new" idea will flop. You see, if you're a fearless entrepreneur, you have been through some flops. If it was easy, everyone would do it. However, those flops are actually great tools and lessons in which to learn and grow from. If you've never had a flop, you've never been a true entrepreneur. We all have flops; it's how we handle those flops that counts. All I can say is make your flops work for you, not against you.

I sometimes find myself wondering what if I had followed my desire right after high school and pursued entrepreneurship. What would my life look like? However, what could have been or might have been isn't very productive. In fact, it lessens the experiences from which I learned and grew. I went on the journey I was meant to go on and all I've endured gave me the life experiences that have allowed me to become an entrepreneur in three businesses today as well as a bestselling author of a few books. What's great is my journey isn't over. It's actually only just begun. Remember that wherever you are, whatever has happened, you are where you are supposed to be!

CHAPTER ELEVEN

~

Fearless Learning: Everything is Solvable

by Kohila Sivas
Founder, MathCodes
www.MathCodes.com

"Among all struggle lies opportunity, but the only way to see it is if we spend time looking for it."
~Kohila Sivas

For the past twenty-two years, I have worked as a math tutor, math teacher, and math coach. I've proven to thousands of struggling students and their parents that anyone can do math. But when I was young, I never dreamed I would be able to help anyone. I really struggled. Oddly, it was math that helped get me through it all.

When I was six years old, my family escaped the civil war in Sri Lanka and emigrated to Canada. It was sudden. On the afternoon I said goodbye to my dear grandparents, I didn't know why they cried. They knew something I did not – that this would be our final embrace. But my dad was determined to get us to safety. And he succeeded.

I thought I knew the meaning of cold, but in Toronto I found out what it really meant. It was like another planet. And we were like aliens. This was truer than it seemed because, at that time, people of colour were treated as invaders.

Then it got worse. Shortly after our arrival in Canada, my father began drinking. His successful business had been burned to the ground, and he had lost everything. It just broke him. Then the abuse began, which sparked more chaos, leading to an abuse on me by a trusted adult.

I felt unsafe at home, but school wasn't any better. I barely spoke a word of English. I was very quiet and intensely shy. The only conversations I had were with myself. Everything was a struggle: language, culture, racism, and life at home.

As a youngster, every day of my life was complicated and out of my control. During this time, I learned to blame myself for everything. By the time I was thirteen, I was exhausted from the pressure – both at home and at school – and wanted nothing more than to stop the pain.

One day, I tried to stop the pain, but was resuscitated in the hospital. Yes, it was that bad.

I went back to school, but my attention would constantly wander, especially during math. I would pretend to be busy by copying the textbook or looking at the posters that hung around my math classroom. I knew them all by heart. One by Albert Einstein read, "*It's not that I'm so smart. It's just that I stay with problems longer.*"

Those words stuck with me. They stirred something deep down inside. Did he really mean that? I began to think of all the things I had given up on, including myself. I started questioning, "How come everyone else could do it, but I couldn't?" I thought that if I let math beat me, I would never become the person I wanted to be.

Finally, after many weeks of consideration, I made up my mind to give it a try. I decided to spend time with math problems.

My teacher noticed my efforts and offered to help. For the very first time, I shared my vulnerability. I opened up and began to ask questions. This was the beginning.

I worked hard, until I could work out smaller problems by myself. I began to fall in love with the process, and with this new feeling of achievement. It was as if I was "hacking the secret codes" of a puzzle. I discovered that my process of reverse engineering and solving math problems seemed SO much simpler than how any teacher explained it. That was when I really started to excel.

My life beyond math was unpredictable, but math gave me confidence. It became therapeutic to me. I would sit for hours and I wouldn't give up. I learned to escape into the world of math and its beauty.

And the feeling was intoxicating. When I worked through a problem, I was in control of everything, from the beginning to the outcome. Because of my success, math helped me break out of my shell.

I began to wonder WHY teachers made math so complicated. And it was that question which inspired me to become a teacher, and later a coach. I knew math could be taught in a simpler way. And I wanted to help students succeed in math just as I had.

My journey to understand math led me to learn that many adults carry the stigma of "failure" in math. Some continue to struggle with that failure throughout their lives. The result is not just a lack of confidence in their own abilities, but worse, doubts about their own intelligence. After all, numbers and words are the basis of our existence. *Therefore*, we figure, *if I can't do math, then I must be dumb.*

That simply is not true.

The truth is this: **anyone can do math given the right environment and the right instruction.** Poor performance is simply the result of poor instruction.

Think back to your own math teachers in school. The good ones knew that it was a system. They didn't skip steps. They enjoyed sharing the beauty of math. Teaching it to others for understanding and appreciation was a joy. That kind of energy lifts and inspires kids to learn.

The right environment has a depth to it that traditional venues simply do not have. It's a fostering environment. It's an environment where coaches don't judge the students, but rather work with them from where they are, not some arbitrary place they are "supposed to be." No child should feel defeated or left behind in any area of education or in life. Every child has the potential to excel.

In 2011, while working as a math teacher and special education assistant in the public education system, I realized that the school environment was not a fit for me. I started investigating what worked and what didn't and started experimenting and finetuning my tutoring process. Along the way, I realized that tutoring methods were old and outdated – it's a trap. Students were trapped in "desperation mode," and I was trapped trading my time for money but not getting anywhere. I was forced to find a way out.

I had to find a way to fight against the status quo of an entire industry.

I decided to stop what I was doing, and to rebuild my process. I needed to create the "right environment" for my tutoring students, and I began to craft a coaching methodology that better supported my students.

Year after year, I continued to develop and test and perfect this methodology by combining math intervention techniques with coaching principles. The result is what I call the MathCodes Diamond system. This system is designed for struggling students, to rebuild their confidence, change their perspectives, and build their performance. In MathCodes coaching, I use math as a vehicle to help students tap into their full potential so they can become fearless lifelong learners.

In 2016, I shifted all my coaching online. It made sense because it supported my goals. I wanted to help more students, but I realized that there was a limit to how much time I had. I was already working at my fullest capacity.

I contemplated hiring other people and training them, but I never liked the model of having employees working with students. A direct relationship between coach and student is necessary for the success of the MathCodes system. I envisioned something special and unique for my students and for the coaches. I also wanted the coaches to be 100% in control of their process and keep 100% of their earnings.

That's when my husband and I landed on training other passionate teachers and tutors under our MathCodes coaching system. We created a certification training program so that all coaches certified by MathCodes can deliver the exact results with their students. With this training, we help the new coach learn the system and run an independent coaching business. We help tutors and teachers escape the "tutoring trap" and gain control over their businesses and their lives.

This has not only given me the opportunity to reach many struggling students beyond what I dreamed, but it has also allowed me to disrupt the broken tutoring industry and establish much-needed standards for the tutoring practice. Now our mission is to reach 50,000 students and certify 1000 coaches all over the world by end of year 2025.

As visionaries, my husband and I are dedicated to making learning math a fearless experience for students and their parents. This exact confidence is what transformed me from a shy, miserable child into a fearless learner, fighter, and coach. I love being an agent of change. I can't wait to certify and connect passionate coaches and experts to the students who need them the most.

Everything is solvable if you spend time with
the problem.
— **Kohila Sivas**

CHAPTER TWELVE

Ghost

by Kristy Boyd Johnson
Boss Lady, Turtle Sea Books
www.TurtleSeaBooks.com

Creativity - like human life itself - begins in darkness.
— **Julia Cameron**

"Goddamn snotnose kids shouldn't be seen or heard," my father would scream at me for the vile crime of – gasp – walking into a room. "Goddamn kids ruin your life."

Yep, I was quite the little hooligan – fingerpainting, reading, watching TV. When would the madness stop?

Wait a sec. Hold on.

I could share my story, tell you all the gory details, but you know what? It's yet another story of yet another abused child who – surprise! – made a lot of mistakes as she dealt with all her inner demons. You've heard it all before, and I don't want to bore you.

What I really want to say is that none of that matters. What really matters is how we use our life experiences to grow, change, and create a good life full of love and friendships. I can't tell you what to do, but I can share a few of the significant things I did to transform my life.

Because I was so emotionally abused, the biggest demon that haunted me was the Shyness Dragon. Even now, I admit, I still struggle with this one quite a bit. Shyness comes from insecurity and a lack of self-worth. It's tough to develop self-worth when you are told how worthless you are every minute of every day. Shyness caused me all kinds of problems over the years, including during the writing of this chapter. I almost didn't do it.

But here goes.

I learned to write early in my twenties. I started writing stories in college and carried that skill into my teaching career. I would make up goofy stories for my kiddoes, and they liked those more than the books on my shelf. So I kept learning, worked at improving my craft.

But, at age 25, I made THE biggest mistake of my life – I got married to a predator who thought he could use my Shyness Dragon to keep me under his thumb and in indentured servitude to his every whim.

Thus began the Coma Years.

For eight nightmarish years, I was lost. I take that back – for seven years I was lost. The eighth year was a year of awakening for me, and reconnecting with my inner Viking warrior woman. And boy, did she come out, sword swinging.

Unfortunately, my renewed spirit and smart mouth caused an escalation of the abuse. I spent many a night locked in the bathroom.

One fine day, I ran. I know beyond all doubt that, had I stayed, I would literally not be alive today. But it had taken me those eight years to get to a place of fearlessness within myself, to an inner place of Light where he could not, and dared not, follow me. And running into the Light felt really good, like I was escaping a vampire.

I spent the next two years trying to get a divorce, without letting him find me. That entire time, I was euphorically happy, even though I was practically destitute. I worked my ass off, re-connected with friends, and just generally enjoyed the peacefulness of living without fear of being punched in the face.

To supplement teaching, I began ghostwriting, and discovered I was good at it. Non-fiction is a whole different animal than fiction, and frankly, much easier. I used ghostwriting to supplement my abysmal teaching income while also working hard to give my clients a unique voice.

But writing is a solitary pursuit and did not trigger the Shyness Dragon to come out and play. Yet I knew it was still there, lying in slumber, just biding its time. Even a party invitation could freak me out. Better to stay home with a hot cup of cocoa, a great book, and my cat purring on my lap.

One day, on a whim, I walked into a Toastmasters meeting and joined the club. Something was awake in me, something urging me to get out there.

In Toastmasters, everyone is required to do an icebreaker speech, which breaks the ice with the group as well as breaking your personal ice on your first speech.

And oh, was my first speech bad. And when I say bad, I mean terrible. Awful. Depressing. Totally sucky.

"How bad?" you ask. Let me tell you.

Bad #1: it was boring as hell – a self-indulgent recitation of a traumatic injury that happened when I was sixteen.

Really, Kristy?

Bad #2: my knees quaked so badly that nearly every comment was, "You were shaking."

Yeah. Thanks. I hadn't noticed.

Bad #3: I cried. Real tears, running down my cheeks. I couldn't help it and couldn't stop it. And they weren't authentic tears from sharing a deeply heartfelt story, oh no. They were the "I'm having a breakdown on the stage" kind that makes one feel like diving into a vat of Valium, and, in the case of one (me) who was attempting to slay the Shyness Dragon, head for the beach and swim out into the vast open ocean, sharks and currents be damned.

But, the Toastmasters, oh, they were gracious. And kind. And lovely. And wonderful. With their love and support, I came back. And I did better on the next speech, and the next, and kept on improving under their guidance, kind comments, and indomitable spirit.

Let me just say, if you want to learn public speaking, go to Toastmasters. They completely rock.

The next thing I did was join an Improv comedy class. I wanted to be able to riff with the audience rather than just memorize my lines. I really admired the seasoned speakers who were able to do that with such ease and confidence and humor.

Improv is a place where the cool kids (aka: nerds. Our respective nerd statuses were discussed. A lot.) let go of all their daily stresses and romp with the other cool kids. The Shyness Dragon retreated a bit during this time, and I began to learn what it was like to relax and enjoy the company of warm, fun, non-judgmental people. Plus, every game, every experience, helped to skyrocket my skills into the stratosphere, and soon I was applying the skills to my speeches.

After some serious nagging… I mean, *encouragement,* my mentor signed me up for a contest. And boom. The Dragon awoke and roared.

But you know what? I did it. And even more freaky – I won.

Back in the real world, I expanded from ghostwriting into editing because, yes, I am one of those obnoxious know-it-alls who mentally corrects grammar, spelling, and punctuation errors. (But not out loud. I'm not *that* insufferable.) Why not get paid for it?

Later, I expanded again, but into book coaching, and that was when I found myself falling into a groove. Coaching allowed me to guide an aspiring author into finding their own authentic voice, rather than me trying to capture it. It's empowering for my clients and a lot more fun for me.

Fast forward to today, with the whole world in flux, including me.

I'm figuring out how to create group classes that are fresh and different from every other writing class out there. I want to do that in conjunction with writing retreats that will give aspiring writers both creative inspiration and concrete, practical advice while also allowing me to satisfy my own wanderlust.

I find joy in empowering my writing clients rather than taking over for them. They get to feel the immense satisfaction that comes from writing, completing, and publishing a book – their own book.

Best of all, my business partner and I are now producing Micro-eBooks for clients. These are short fiction or non-fiction books of 10,000 words or fewer and can be used in so many amazing ways: lead magnets, supplemental materials like workbooks, coloring books, children's books, journals – pretty much whatever you can imagine.

It's fun for us, and exciting for our clients who don't have to assassinate their budgets in order to create amazing materials to ramp up their businesses.

In all honesty, I haven't slain the Shyness Dragon. The best I can claim is that it's lulled to sleep and a spirit of adventure has awakened. When it comes to this, it's one day at a time.

I can live with that.

The road to hell is paved with adverbs.
— **Stephen King**

CHAPTER THIRTEEN

~

Boldly Embracing Fearlessness to EMERGE

by Krystylle Richardson
CEO, Life Innovation, Woman Weekend-Preneur
www.KrystylleRichardson.com

Let's go on a little journey. First stop is "understanding."

Before I say anything, I want to start with a few personal definitions. The word fearless to me means one who is without limits. Entrepreneur means one who believes in oneself enough to go out and do whatever it takes to make their dreams a reality and, as a bonus, get paid for doing so. Putting those two together this is what I get: A limitless minded person who has the bold tenacity to go and build legacy. From here forward I will use the initials F.E. to term "fearless entrepreneur."

With that definition in mind, I consider myself to be a fearless entrepreneur. I consider myself a person who is one who thrives in life daily helping to build the next F.E.

Next stop on this journey is "what we allow."

I let fear of failure, fear of success, and fear of the unknown control me for too long. I let my run-away thoughts about what others thought about me control my next steps. Fear is huge and does not have to be. We give it the power it has and we can just as easily smash the power under our feet. For years I let fear control my mind just like a cigarette does for those who are addicted (from what I understand). It is my hope that this chapter gives you extra insight into how you can move forward past your fears and create the life you deserve as the next biggest, baddest entrepreneur.

Let's take another step on this journey to "self-discovery and self-value." I recently created and hosted a really cool media experience called EMERGE. The word is also an acronym with a broader meaning. EMERGE stands for E-Energize, M-Move, E-Evolve and Endure, R-Rise, and E-Encourage self and others. We all have the ability to emerge as the next top entrepreneur in our field, but are we willing to do what it takes to get there. Are we surrounding ourselves with thought leaders and mentors. Surrounding yourself with people who believe in you and who you can support is key. Emerge was about understanding the links of relationship and how we can create something great for people to get a glimpse into our character and our value. To be fearless also means that we have to value ourselves, value our thoughts, and not just look for validation. When I think of the F.E. and the fact that I was asked to be a part of this amazing project by Lynda Sunshine, it made me feel so special. Why? Because this means that something I have either both said and done caused her to see that spark in me. As mentioned earlier, though, we have to value ourselves. Value our sparks and our own inner beauty. So I have a question for you. What sparks do you see in yourself and in others? Do you see a bright, bright burning light that is fearful or one that is fearless? Our light attracts energy and creates a forcefield of hope or despair.

So I ask you, what type of fort or forcefield are you building? What energy are you radiating? Do people see the urgency in your actions, the fire and power in your voice, and the burning desire in your spirit to be the best version of self? If you know that you have honestly evaluated yourself, you know whether or not you are giving your all, doing your best, being the person that you want to look up to. Are you ok with what you see in the mirror? All of these self-evaluations are ones I am noting because they are ones that I had to do on myself. I still do them daily. When I go to sleep I do my best to go to sleep empty. This means that I gave my all that day. I wake up with the fire of purpose to no longer let fear and the unknown and what-ifs take over my mind and my behavior. This is so, so easy to do, let me tell you. I did it for years and the outcome is not a good one. I allowed other people's expectations of me to drive my daily existence. I let pleasing people be the focus rather than please myself and God most of all. I let my hope to be accepted in all circles drive me to tears and not being my authentic self in most of those same circles. I tried to fit into circles rather than being ok to step back and take a look at my giftings and building my own circles, bringing my own seat to the table, and building my own ladders.

Let's get to the mountain-top experience of the journey and go to "building our fearless toolkit." I let fear rob me for too long. I let fear stop me from gaining the access that I was already granted by God to have massive impact in this world. I let fear stop me from being my unique version of great. I implore you to never ever follow in my footsteps in this manner. How much time did I waste? How many lives did I not save because I selfishly followed fear vs following my dreams?

You see, we all have greatness inside of us just aching and sometimes oozing as it tries to get out, but we hold it in.

Because of the troubles and triumphs I have had in my life, I would like to take the rest of this time to share a few struggles and methods of triumph with you to use the remainder of my section of this amazing collection.

1. Krystylle's trouble: Allowing fear to drive my world

Krystylle's tip to turn trouble to triumph: Be fearless in your entrepreneurial walk by being intentional in your thoughts. Your thoughts control your actions. Drive your thoughts with verbal cues to yourself as needed until you can successfully drive them in your head without audible cues.

2. Krystylle's trouble: Focusing too much on clients' plans vs my own

Krystylle's tip to turn trouble to triumph: Be fearless in your entrepreneurial walk by never allowing your goals to take a back seat. Press forward intentionally on your own timelines and schedule time for self. If you leave you out, it will show in the long run and you will burn out. Failure happens oftentimes when we feel that we have nothing left to give. Put yourself first.

3. Krystylle's trouble: Not accepting self as being a fierce force of nature

Krystylle's tip to turn trouble to triumph: Be fearless in your entrepreneurial walk by agreeing with yourself that you are an expert, you are powerful, you are a person to be listened to, you have what it takes. The flip side of this is to not just say it, but to do the behind-the-scenes work needed to make your words true. Spend the time with self and with fortifying your fortress. Be willing to invest in yourself as a force of nature.

4. Krystylle's trouble: Being pre-occupied with money vs wealth

Krystylle's tip to turn trouble to triumph: Be fearless in your entrepreneurial walk by understanding your relationship with money. Money is a vehicle and not a blockage. Oftentimes we do things to get the next dollar rather than looking at our lives long term. Create and build on a wealth strategy not just the next paycheck. Multiple streams of income is a necessary part of it. My first 6 figures, then next and next and next, moving into 7-figure territory year after year has come from numerous streams. Build your streams and keep them wet with innovation. Doing things the same way over and over works in some cases and others not so much. Be open to new things and keep the foundational elements that work and innovate the rest.

5. Krystylle's trouble: Not speaking up about what I believe in

Krystylle's tip to turn trouble to triumph: Be fearless in your entrepreneurial walk by being true to you and your morals, values and even some of your strong opinions. Wise can be spoken when you are able to verbalize experiences. Being fearless on this journey takes you sometimes getting exactly what you want by speaking up and also being turned away for it. That is ok. It is better to stand for something than to be tossed with the wind and being left empty.

6. Krystylle's trouble: Allowing the safety of corporate life stifle my risk taking for greater gains

Krystylle's tip to turn trouble to triumph: Be fearless in your entrepreneurial walk by embodying the word fearless. Corporations are good for lots of folks to have stability. If you have a personal burning desire in your soul to do something more, though, then you MUST, and yes I said MUST, go for it. Living in the woulda, shoulda, coulda is a death sentence. I have been there and it is not fun. I am grateful that I am able to still help as needed in corporate environments as well as with the one-on-one newbie entrepreneur that wants to spread their wings and fly.

7. Krystylle's trouble: Being ok as a copycat and not an original in some areas of life

Krystylle's tip to turn trouble to triumph: Be fearless in your entrepreneurial walk by owning your uniqueness. We were all created differently to serve different purposes on this earth.

In conclusion, I am thankful that this little girl from Flint Michigan finally figured that out and is well on her way to continue to impact nature, one person at a time on this journey called life.

How about you, are you ready to do the same?

Let's be fearless together. Let's all discover and master our true freedom formulas and our Financial Independence Preparedness Plans (FIPP™). I love helping people through my Life Innovation initiatives to unleash their freedom formulas and discover the joy and freedom of life as they discover untapped-income they never knew they had. Money does not buy happiness. What it does do is it makes our time that God gave us on this earth easier to navigate as we pour into others, do you agree? Thank you for taking this journey with me; let's be that future self we are working towards. Let's go.

CHAPTER FOURTEEN

❧

The Seven Promises of COURAGE!™ for Entrepreneurs

by Kym Glass
CEO, Soft Skills Strategies
www.KymGlass.com

I remember leaving my corporate career of 20+ years and launching out to become an entrepreneur. One day while working in my own office and looking at my blank calendar I thought, how was I able to effortlessly get all of my tasks done while being the go-to-person for over 3,500 employees in our corporate division?

That thought immediately got me into action to begin figuring out how to work my entrepreneur schedule and booking it full with calls, producing networking events, completing operational activities and ultimately building several connected communities of like-minded entrepreneurs.

As an entrepreneur, it is important to leverage your skills and abilities to be in a place of continuous learning while also taking action toward the various tasks. My Dad was a custom home builder and I learned by watching him as he continuously honed his skills in every area of the custom home process. He didn't actually do all of the tasks, but he knew what was needed and how to leverage the best experts to get the work done.

Compared to what you can really accomplish in your life as an entrepreneur, it is not just skills and abilities that get you there. What I've learned in consulting with many entrepreneurs and their teams is what really gets in the way are irrational fears that hold them back.

Is there something calling you to step up your leadership as an entrepreneur, but you are not sure how to get there? Oftentimes an irrational fear, a holdback or something that you may not recognize, prevents us from moving up to a more powerful place. Irrational fear can impact our confidence, productivity, and even our collaboration efforts.

How would you feel if you were more confident as an entrepreneur? What could you REALLY accomplish if you had more skills or abilities to gain momentum? What results would be possible if you were working in a flow instead of holding yourself back?

Imagine 84% of people hold onto an irrational fear that is keeping them awake at night and preventing them from being successful in their personal and/or business life. From my own experiences, I have found to move through fear with COURAGE is the key to gaining clarity of the root cause.

I know what it feels like to live in fear. I was born into and raised in a religious cult. Because of the fear I felt of the leaders; I lost my parents, I lost my freedom, and I lost myself for 35 years! In order to break free, escape, and ultimately protect my own daughter and future generations, I knew I must muster up the COURAGE to break free. This breaking free stemmed from a four-generational pattern that had preyed on my family and I was determined to achieve my goal of FEARLESS FREEDOM!

Looking back and realizing that even though that one area of my life was so overwhelmed with fear, I was miraculously able to excel in my corporate career and then as an entrepreneur. The belief that I could own my effort and take consistent initiative through self-leadership to accomplish any goal was what I thrived on.

Imagine yourself as an entrepreneur with the resources, tools and support to get you where you want to go. Here is a simple and quick assessment quiz to help you gain clarity.

Are You Living In Fear As an Entrepreneur.….. Take the Quiz!

1. I am afraid to pick up the phone and make calls for my business.
2. I am scared that I will make a wrong business decision.
3. I am scared that other people will not agree with my opinions.
4. I am scared that I will not be liked by others.
5. I am afraid of losing my business.
6. I am scared and unsure of what and how to talk to others about my business.
7. I am afraid to promote my business on social media.
8. I am afraid I will be criticized for my appearance.
9. I am scared of sharing my business and being rejected by others.
10. I won't try because I'm afraid I'll fail.

_____ Total # of Yes answers.

- Hey, if you answered 1 question Yes, we are all human. ☺
- If you answered 2 questions with Yes, you are very likely living in fear as an entrepreneur.

- If you answered 3+ questions with Yes, I'm sorry to tell you, but you are living your life in major fear as an entrepreneur and you need to learn to be **BRAVE!**

The Daily Dose of B-R-A-V-E!

B – Believe in yourself! It is the very foundation where your confidence lies. Pour your focus and energy into believing in yourself for anything you want to accomplish. Do you recognize any negative thoughts, ideas, behaviors or patterns that are not representing you as your most powerful self?

R – Roadmap. Create the map you need to keep you on course and navigate yourself away from any fear.

A – Abilities. Use your own abilities and learn new abilities to help you move through your fear. What if your focus was more about what you "want and deserve" instead of what you feel or think you lack?

V – View. The only view that you need to focus on are your goals. Do you spend time every day encouraging yourself with the vision you have of your entrepreneur goals?

E – Expectations. Forget about everyone else's expectations for you and your life, and demand what you want for yourself and/or your family. How would you feel if you were able to flip the negative story you've been listening to from either yourself or others and make them positive toward your expectations?

After taking the first step of gaining clarity, facing reality, and becoming BRAVE, I realized those insights could springboard me to a higher level and ultimately to live with power.

From this new point of view, "The Seven Promises of COURAGE!" ™ Roadmap was created.

The Seven Promises of COURAGE!

The 1ˢᵗ Promise of C̲OURAGE:
Confidence - Believe in Yourself.

When you are confident within yourself and have belief in yourself, you become unstoppable. It is the very foundation of your belief system that everything else is built upon. As an entrepreneur, if you do not believe in yourself, how can others believe in you to help them?

The 2nd Promise of COURAGE:
Ownership - Be in the Driver's Seat of Your Own Life.

Self-ownership is crucial to your journey as an entrepreneur. When you are in the driver's seat of your life, you are confident and take charge of your own direction. Open the door, step inside, and rest comfortably in the driver's seat of your life and business as an entrepreneur.

The 3rd Promise of COURAGE:
Unstoppable - Trust Your Inner Power.

When you are operating from an unstoppable place, you are moving through with great energy, aliveness, and COURAGE that is unexplainable. You are no longer distracted by excuses, other people's opinions, or any holdbacks as they relate to what you need to do in order to become a successful entrepreneur because your day is so booked that distractions are easily avoided.

The 4th Promise of COURAGE:
Relationships - Create Your Connected Community.

Relationships are so incredibly important and even more so as an entrepreneur. There are so many groups, associations, and various communities to be a part of and also support. Healthy relationships are paramount to aiding and inspiring you toward your goals as an entrepreneur.

The 5th Promise of COURAGE:
Action - Take a Different Action for a Different Result.

It is only in taking action upon an idea, tackling a project, and making a decision toward the result you want that change happens. Look real close into your business as an entrepreneur, where are the gaps that you see that with more action you could achieve better results?

The 6th Promise of COURAGE:
Gratitude - The Gateway to Your Desires.

Gratitude is the gateway to anything you truly desire. When you are grateful, it becomes the opening for unexpected miracles to appear. Are you grateful that you are an entrepreneur with what sets your heart and soul on fire?

The 7th Promise of COURAGE:
Empowered - Helping Others From Who You Are.

Being empowered about a vision and mission bigger than you is so inspiring. By digging deep within yourself, being brave and having COURAGE, you can live your life from WHO you are and help others from a higher level.

In my personal journey of 35 years of consistent and unrelenting tearful, bullying, and toxic experiences, once I was able to recognize the generational pattern trap I was in, I was finally able to break free from the beliefs and opinions of others that no longer served me.

The journey as an entrepreneur is not linear; it is more likened to a roller coaster. As you become more aware and continue to fine tune what no longer serves you, you can begin to live with power and become an entrepreneur full of COURAGE!

I challenge you to give yourself grace to learn and grow. In doing so, you will be able to move through any fear with COURAGE knowing that you will land safely on the other side because you chose to move forward in growth.

CHAPTER FIFTEEN

~

The Pandemic Pivot of 2020

by Lois Koffi
Founder, Lois Koffi Enterprises
www.LoisKoffi.com

It was the best of times, it was the worst of times, it was the
age of wisdom, it was the age of foolishness, it was the epoch
of belief, it was the epoch of incredulity, it was the season of
light, it was the season of darkness, it was the spring of hope,
it was the winter of despair.
— Charles Dickens, *A Tale of Two Cities*

I felt like the Universe had bitch-slapped me into waking up from a long dream-like state. I started 2020 like the last several years, very "busy" and consumed by making money and chasing the seemingly elusive dream – freedom.

I went on exhaustive and, at times, thankless business trips and poured myself into people without seeing immediate fruit.

Ironically, it was the bondage of the unforeseen pandemic shut down in the third month of 2020 that gave me what I had been seeking relentlessly for several years.

Permission to Find Freedom

I had been on autopilot without even realizing it, working 7 days a week for years – a pursuit that was modeled to me by those around me in multiple sales focused organizations. I had the belief that working HARD meant I would succeed much bigger, much faster, and had lost sight of what I previously knew to be true.

Being in the Flow Is True Freedom

I learned about "the flow" during the Great Recession of 2006-08. I lost everything during those years, after multiple six figures success, global travel and being an Ironman Triathlete.

Yet, when I had my car repossessed on August 31, 2007, the day before my 30th birthday, I didn't freak out.

All else had been "lost" or taken. Foreclosure and bank accounts being cleaned out – while traumatic as a first-time event – didn't kill my Spirit.

It didn't matter – I wasn't deterred. I chalked it up as an Experience.

I stayed in the flow and trusted the Universe would take care of me. Somewhere along the way, I had forgotten and lost sight of this "flow."

A lot changed now that I had two mouths to feed and my husband lost his job.

A lot changed when something deep inside of me became scared and fed into the lie of fear.

That was when I immersed myself into autopilot and "running" 7 days a week.

Years later, when the world "paused" (in what some call the "Big Pause" of 2020), I woke up to some new (or old) realizations.

I could finally slow down enough to smell the proverbial coffee.

There has been a lot of loss this year for many. I was ONLY able to pivot quickly because of my previous experience in 2007-08, when I became homeless and lost everything I had (including my health).

I was not unfamiliar with being hit hard – and quickly knew what to do. (This was even with having my brother and mom die unexpectedly in February and April, losing two other family members, two friends committing suicide, and another friend, who appeared to be the picture of health, died of cancer. None of these were Covid-19 related and all were in 2020.)

All of these events, on top of the pandemic, caused me to slow down.

To reflect.

AND also to realize no one succeeds (or fails) alone.

That was when I decided to pivot.

I took the pain of the earlier events in the year and hired a new coach that could help me launch my podcast. I transmuted that pain into creative writing and speaking – sharing my heart and my message.

I decided to be vulnerable and share my grief, as opposed to stuff it down as I had done so well two years prior when my Dad died suddenly.

Growing up in a German/Dutch household, I learned a lot about stuffing down emotions and just keep moving forward. Being vulnerable was not trained, even in the church I went to as a kid.

I am grateful I released that lack of vulnerability – that judgment I had passed on so many for so long.

Showing tears and grief and vulnerability is NOT a weakness. Neither is asking for help or admitting weaknesses.

I found by sharing my story, I gave people permission to share theirs and to connect deeply with me.

I found that people trusted me as a result of speaking my own truth.

The irony of all ironies…after years of working my ass off 7 days a week, up at dawn and down at dusk EVERY single day…I started making more money than I had made in the past 13 years.

I returned to making the income I had made when I was selling real estate.

In the years I was "in the flow" of service and allowing people and opportunity to come to me.

In the years where I didn't work nights or weekends and had hobbies and friendships outside of work – where I didn't even try to mix business and pleasure… although it did happen after the fact.

In the years when I just focused on being my authentic self and simply connected with people, meeting them where they were.

It was effortless.

Only this was even better than that – I found my purpose – my Calling, if you will.

I found Wisdom and it was fun.

My coach encouraged me to take more time off (which was the opposite approach I previously experienced with mentors/business partners).

I reluctantly took off Sundays…and the money kept flowing in. I didn't even think about it. It just flowed.

Taking that one day off didn't hurt me.

In fact, quite the opposite…it started a healing process I didn't even realize I needed.

Despite the pain and grieving process I was enduring with my therapist, the Universe was providing for me and my family.

I had to laugh…it took several people dying and a pandemic shut down to get my attention.

One must ask, why do humans need to be so stubborn?

Why do we allow ourselves to be brainwashed by society and others who teach us to cope and medicate ourselves with workaholism and "running" through life?

I read the book *The Surrender Experiment* by Michael Alan Singer during the fourth quarter of 2020 and it made me cry tears of relief.

I have finally surrendered…and it feels so fucking good.

I didn't realize how much "weight" I was carrying on my back (oh, and not to mention I've gained 30 pounds since my dad died over two years ago…coincidence?).

No matter how lost we become in life – surrounded by those who might be leading us astray from our own core values and beliefs – there is always an opportunity to surrender and come back to center. To listen to that still, small voice within. To come back to ourselves. Our true Self.

What has 2020 meant for you?

I realize this chapter may be read many years or decades from now. It doesn't matter.

We are always facing our own self-imposed pandemic (as I had in the Great Recession).

2020 isn't the only example of waking ourselves up.

At any time you can have an Awakening of sorts (an epiphany that course-corrects your chosen path, even if that path appears to be the road less traveled).

What does one do with Self-Realization?

How does one pivot back to Center?

Here are a few tips I find helpful for pivoting and living my BEST life – no matter what storm is traversing around me.

1. Stop and listen to the silence. Slow down more and find 5 to 10 minutes a day of stillness. Regroup. Recenter. Reflect.
2. Journal your thoughts. Getting things out on paper (yes, the old school handwriting kind) can awaken the subconscious. Seeing what we write on paper can be enlightening to what is really going on within.

3. Have a conversation with a mentor or a coach who can give subjective advice – giving yourself permission to have a third party who has your best interest at heart (choose wisely) can prevent self-sabotage.

4. Do less – BE more. Take a freaking break. Take time off. LIVE and not just become a human DOING. So many people want your time. Tell them to take a flying leap if they keep persisting and it doesn't resonate with you…setting those BEING boundaries will change your life and are actually something you have control over (we can't control people).

5. Speak your truth. Ask for what you want. Be vulnerable. Shooting straight with people is empowering. Too many years I held back my truth (and manifested an autoimmune disease in my throat – no kidding). People appreciate honesty more than you know. People-pleasing and co-dependency is no longer on my to-do list.

Here's to your success in pivoting.

Coach Lois

This chapter is dedicated to my husband Didier, our kids David, Henry and Desiree, and all those who supported me this year.

To my brother Rich and our Mom Albertha – your passing taught me so much about grace and love.

And all the Souls in 2020 who were lost and those who were left behind to grieve.

May you find your FLOW amidst the pain.

CHAPTER SIXTEEN

~

The Fear of Being Lola

by Lola Oyafemi
Founder, Lola Oyafemi Consulting
www.LolaOyafemi.com

The worst person to lie to is yourself.

And that's what I have been doing for the last couple of months. I had abandoned the truth I believed in and started claiming to be someone that I was not. I sat down and painted a picture so fake that I have chased it consistently without stopping. And I'm not alone. So many people in the coaching world lie about stuff...

About the money we make... our choices... our relationships....

And we do it because of fear.... The fear of judgment, the fear of competition, the fear of people finding out...

We become the imposter... Fearful Entrepreneurs. We overemphasize our success and hide our failures beneath.

How do I know this? Because this is where I am.

When I spoke to Lynda Sunshine about my chapter, I wanted to talk about impact. But, as I listened to Nicole Cherie Baker's podcast on lying, I realized that the number 1 thing stopping me from impact is my fear.

My fear of being Lola....

Because beneath that fear is my true power and it's the same with you.

I just had a failed launch. It's not my first failed launch and it will probably not be my last....

Have I had clients succeed? Yes. Have I had clients struggle? Yes.

Imagine if I shared everything I learned from my flops and how to move forward... I bet I would have made more impact.

Those 'fake it till you make it' posts that remove all semblance of authenticity from social media… are no longer necessary.

There's no veil I have to hide behind… I can proclaim the truth and I will.

That's the true making of a fearless entrepreneur.

Someone who isn't afraid to be their true self. Success and Failure Combined.

That person who refuses to let failure define who they are or what they become. Now this isn't some self-help chapter where I give you a list of meditations or some affirmations.

No, I'll do better than that. I will be Lola for real... the blunt Lola and tell you how it is.

Look at yourself in the mirror and tell yourself the truth. Confront the lies you have said so many times that you've started believing them to be true.

And not just money lies. Is your health where you want it to be?

On a scale of 1 to 10, are your relationships as happy as you claim on social media?

Do an audit. I did one this afternoon and I realized the only reason I hired 3 people wasn't because I was ready, but because I kept lying to myself about my finances.

As I did this audit, I saw a clear pattern on how to move forward. The true way to let go of that fear is to be brutally honest with yourself... in my case I have a good business but I'm still tied to it. The two months I was ill, I made no money yet I hired people thinking that was the solution.

But once I took the audit, I realized the reason I was struggling was because I had become the bottleneck of my business. I wasn't consistent and I kept a Facebook group that was no longer serving me.

First thing I did was to outsource to my employees immediately, then archive my Facebook group (I'll rebrand and renew my commitment to the group in the coming weeks).

All in a day's work because I told myself the truth and I'm writing this chapter almost immediately after.

And I'm not ashamed to share this because that's what being fearless truly is.

Now it's your turn.

Where have you been hiding?

In what area do you pretend to be someone else?

Where are you stuck comparing yourself to other people?

Be brutally honest with yourself today so you can look that fear in the face and kick it.

Then you can be truly Fearless.

When you get to the stage of being Fearless, the first thing you'll notice is Freedom.

You see, right from childhood, most of us have been conditioned to be afraid. It starts as fear from your parents

'Don't run off the stairs.'

'Stop, you will fall down.'

'That dog will bite you.'

Then it graduates to fear of not belonging in school. We are taught to be a copy of everyone else. 'That's not how good girls behave,' 'Boys don't cry,' 'You can only succeed if you go to college.'

When we didn't conform, we got detention, punishment, and, in some cases like mine -- beaten with a cane, belt, slippers, or pretty much anything.

Eventually, we start living with the fear of being ourselves because we have been punished so many times for being different.

So our first step in any system is to look for validation from other people....

When we see that our ideas or plans look different from other people, we begin to conform.

We adopt a Herd Mentality — The tendency for people's behaviors or beliefs to conform to those of the group to which they belong.

In the words of Fashion Designer, Vivienne Westwood — 'We are the most amazing creatures that this world has ever produced, but we seem to also have this herd mentality; we seem to be the most stupid, also.'

In business, that herd mentality is keeping you from being truly fearless.

So your offer is like every other offer in the marketplace, your social media is the same... You are a copy of gurus and other businesses.

But, you know deep down that you are not designed to be a copy... You are original.

You are Fearless and You are ready to make an impact.

You are no longer going to be an imitation.

You accept your uniqueness and your powerful individuality.

It's your time.

Do an audit of your life and be brutally honest.

Identify where you have been afraid of being judged... See the areas where you have been lying and exaggerating.

Decide to move on from that fear.... Start showing up as yourself.

Don't be a copy when you can shine in your true form and be strong.

THE FEARLESS ENTREPRENEURS

Talk about your failures and talk about your successes.... Let people see your rollercoaster ride and show them how you make it different.

This won't be the longest chapter in this book or even the most insightful... that's not the goal.

The goal of this chapter is for you to embrace the real you, the true you behind the glimmer, the strategies, the successes and the failures.

And it's okay not be perfect. It's okay to be a mess. It's okay to have storms and not all rainbows.

It is okay to be You...

Because only then do you become fearless.

Only then do you become the Fearless Entrepreneur that changes the world.

Love,

Lola Oyafemi.

> p.s. "Our deepest fear is not that we are inadequate. Our deepest fear is that we are powerful beyond measure. It is our light, not our darkness, that most frightens us. We ask ourselves, 'Who am I to be brilliant, gorgeous, talented, fabulous?' Actually, who are you not to be? You are a child of God. Your playing small does not serve the world. There is nothing enlightened about shrinking so that other people won't feel insecure around you. We are all meant to shine, as children do. We were born to make manifest the glory of God that is within us. It's not just in some of us; it's in everyone. And as we let our own light shine, we unconsciously give other people permission to do the same. As we are liberated from our own fear, our presence automatically liberates others."
>
> ~ Marianne Williamson, *A Return to Love: Reflections on the Principles of "A Course in Miracles"*

CHAPTER SEVENTEEN

~

Where Are You on Your Journey?

by Marilen Crump
Founder, ARTINSPIRED, LLC
www.MarilenCrump.com

We all start the same... as little innocent beings with only instincts to guide our reactions. But somewhere down the path, we develop into a new awareness, and FEAR is introduced into how we live our lives. Since this is a book about being "fearless," I need to first define what it means in my vocabulary - what words do I use to describe that about myself. Well, here's what is coming to mind: Confident, Bold, Attuned, Decisive, Independent, Assured, Self-Trusting, Faithful, and Passionate.

When I read those words, a big part of me definitely resonates with it, but there is a small hesitation that lurks in the corner of my mind. We all have that element of self-doubt, which I think is a good counterpoint to always being too self-assured. It is okay to keep in touch with the humbling points that outer circumstances bring to our daily lives like mistakes, confusion, and frustration. After all, we are all human.

The biggest recollection of fear that I remember as a child was feeling pain and anxiousness as four of my front teeth were in advanced stages of rotting. We lived in the Philippines where I was born into poverty and my parents were struggling to provide for our family. I was six years old and I remember laying in my sweat as fever was taking over my body due to the state of my teeth. I didn't know if I was going to make it. I thought to myself that if I lived through this moment, that I would do whatever it took to be worthy of it. To this day, I think about how the desperation advanced me emotionally and mentally. Would I have been thinking those thoughts if that episode never occurred? Do six-year-olds think that way normally? I was literally in fear of dying and the physical feeling was forcing that upon me.

We moved and lived in various places as a military family. Germany was one of my favorites and the food was amazing. By the time middle school rolled around, we were naturalized citizens of the United States and I was going through the phases of adolescence. I went from being carefree to being afraid of disappointing people, began thinking of my future - things like college and career. I looked around at the adults in my life and they did not seem very happy. They looked exhausted and worried about money.

By the time I was in high school, I would figure out ways to use my talents to earn money. I was fortunate that my father gave me one of his film cameras to use and I quickly learned how to create headshots that would help my acting friends get booked for gigs. All of this would morph into creating my business ARTINSPIRED, which I officially branded my senior year of college.

I made a promise to myself that once I graduated, that I would continue my path of the "entrepreneurial creative" despite all the negative responses I received from my parents. They were afraid that I would not be successful. They had seen others fail in their lives and automatically expressed that it was a foolish way to go through life. I was torn but, thankfully, stubborn enough to keep going. They had no concept of how hard-working I was or how personable I could be when selling my skills and services to others. I did have a few positions that helped supplement my lifestyle - I was a Web Designer for a Non-Profit Association, taught Ballroom Dance for two studios, did graphic design for an Automotive Toy Company, performed in Professional Theatre, Acted in Commercials, Film and Television, and was a Print Model. I did pretty much anything that was fun and creative.

I was FEARLESS!

I learned that rejection was a part of the process. I realized that you can keep growing and achieving new levels of success when you are focused on your dreams.

I felt invincible and yet my parents' disappointment would start infiltrating my confidence. I did not want them to stop loving me and that was my biggest fear. I was also getting very lonely in my freelance existence. I always had to explain to people why I didn't have a full-time job or benefits. Was all of it going to end one day and I would be unprepared for a solid career?

I began dating a guy that seemed to have it all figured out. He was six years younger than me, but my parents really liked what he was about. I began to think that maybe they were all correct about their perspective of life. They also kept mentioning how much they loved me, but I was being difficult and stubborn. I never wanted to be called those things and it made me sad. I was sad enough that I began to transform myself to their liking. I got married and right away became pregnant with my first child.

It was a miserable time for me. Motherhood felt like an anchor where my family would use it to guilt me to stop trying to be a freelancer. I felt trapped and the rift was too much. By the time I had my second child, the marriage was in shambles and we eventually divorced. Through all of the depressing moments of those years, I began to shift back into being a business leader. It was something that gave me confidence. God gets all the credit for this part as he sent me an amazing soulmate - my TRUE LOVE - Kenny. We were instant friends and he believed in me and what I had to offer the world.

My entrepreneurial life is so ingrained in my heart that it really takes a true advocate to have as a life partner. We got married with our eyes wide open and every day I know I am treasured and supported. He was the person that introduced me to the Law of Attraction and enriched my spiritual path. All the lessons we learn together are to be shared with others. I am a better leader because of it.

I have made many bold changes to my business with this strong foundation of love and wisdom. The fear of not being enough no longer haunts me. I am able to encourage others on their path and coach many entrepreneurs on how they can shift their mindset. I created the D.R.E.A.M. Success Strategy and am known as an "Expert Dream Catcher." ARTINSPIRED is now a source for Business Development, Marketing Strategy, Online Platform, and Community Design, as well as creating an organization called "Phenomenal Female Business Network."

If there is anything I can tell you about being a FEARLESS EN-TREPRENEUR it would be that you must stay true to your purpose. I feel such joy in my heart when I get to serve using the gifts I have been blessed with. I am able to make MORE MONEY and meet amazing people all over the globe.

I was recently given the honor of being a commencement speaker for a local college where I was able to speak about embracing change. What we definitely know in business is that there are no certainties. The only thing you can rely on is being able to think fast and transact often. Remember these two things: PERFECTIONISM is a Trap and Fail among people who LOVE you. When you hold that statement in your soul - there is nothing you should fear.

YOU DESERVE TO LIVE YOUR DREAMS.

YOU CAN CREATE YOUR FUTURE.

Life is still evolving for me and there are still lessons to learn. I strongly encourage you to develop your INTUITION. Each morning is an opportunity to clear your head from any old concerns, meditate on new possibilities, and craft a solid action plan. Confidence is a muscle that has to be exercised. I am thankful for those who are in my life that continue to inspire me. I also want to dedicate this chapter to Lynda Sunshine West who is a gift in my life. Thank you, Lynda, for your beautiful heart.

CHAPTER EIGHTEEN

~

Life After Brain Cancer

By Mark Ledlow
in loving memory of my loving dad,
Terry David Ledlow
Host, The Fearless Mindset Podcast
www.fearlessmindsetpodcast.com

D ad had been motionless all day with barely enough energy
to breathe. It was May Day 2019, the day he was placed in
hospice care. My sisters were holding his hands and I had my
arm around his shoulders. I was falling apart inside as I watched him
just lay there, questioning if I had done enough to save him from the
brain cancer. It had been an excruciatingly long four years with that
diagnosis.

I believe Dad could hear my sisters sobbing uncontrollably as I was
"trying" to be the calm one telling him, "It's okay if you want to leave
us and join Mom up in heaven." As he lay there, I reminded him he
was mere seconds away from having a perfected body. Dad had been a

pastor and in his belief system he knew his eternal life was much greater than his life here on earth.

Right before he took his last breath, it was as if a paramedic used AED pads to shock him back to life. He jolted up, opened his eyes, and made eye contact with each one of us there in the room. It made no difference that he had gone blind a few weeks prior. Dad was smiling with such love. He took one big breath, and although he said "Help," I am assured that what he really meant to say was, "I love you guys and I'll see you in heaven." He knew his next breath would be in the presence of his Lord and Savior, and he would be reunited with his beautiful bride once again.

I had never watched someone pass away. I stood there in shock, processing the moment. I was exhausted. I heard a quiet voice reassure me, "Mark, your dad is up in heaven right now, celebrating and having the time of his life." I was in a fog of grief, feeling numb for the next few years. I had just lost my dad, my best friend. The shock deeply challenged my own identity. Who was I now?

I had just spent the past four years as the full-time caregiver for my dad, taking him to endless doctor appointments, in and out of hospitals, even pulling him out of nursing homes without doctor releases. I saw firsthand the neglect our nation's elderly experience in our medical system. It made me sick to my stomach and I made a decision that there was NO WAY my dad would be treated like that. After having lived in nursing homes with him, I now deeply respected the cultures that believe in taking care of their own elderly parents. I witnessed that 90% of residents of the nursing homes and rehabilitation centers were not visited by their own families. This was very troubling to me.

Perhaps you are wondering how I was able to do all of this and continue to work at the same time. I often wondered that myself. Here's the simple answer. In my mid-20s, I crossed paths with some multi-millionaires whom I actually thought had some crazy ideas, but I listened and learned many basic business concepts from them. The most profound one was the understanding that no amount of money can buy back time. After spending those four years with my dad, I can honestly say they were absolutely correct.

Having been exposed to these businessmen and businesswomen, receiving both mentorship and coaching, I realized I needed to retrain my brain from a "W2 Mindset" to an "Owner Mindset." These are two distinctly different mindsets and it required years of personal growth to develop those mental muscles. It also took trial-and-error to create a level of belief that you can actually create a business.

I read books, listened to audios, attended leadership conferences, changed my daily habits, and heeded the guidance of my mentors. I learned quickly by asking myself, "Am I going to listen to my job-brain to build a business or am I going to listen to a mentor who has fruit on his/her tree—a mentor who has 'been there and done that'?" Mentors can save you thousands of hours and dollars in mistakes. Pride will cost you thousands, if not millions, of dollars and hours in losses. Interestingly, Dad had taught me Proverbs 16:18 "Pride goeth before destruction, and a haughty spirit before a fall." Gaining control of "time" became the foundation of my success, allowing me to spend those four years with my dad during his most difficult time on earth.

Years earlier, I worked four seasons as a wildland firefighter with the Oregon Department of Forestry. Dad had convinced me to try the military. I thought long and hard about the idea, studying each branch closely to see which I would benefit from the most. The Marines. That was my decision. Even knowing the reputation of the Marine Corps bootcamp being hell on earth, I signed up. And it was hell. And it gave me the fire I would draw on for the rest of my life. It gave me the brotherhood that would open doors I had never dreamed of. Any fears I ever had in my life were purged from my soul during my time in the

Marine Corps (with the exception of losing my dad to cancer. Nothing can prepare you for that.)

My experiences in the Marine Corps unlocked a psychological block in my mind: "There was nothing I could not do." My experiences in law enforcement and corrections, then working in corporate America in sales and finance and banking would prepare me for the ultimate crash in 2008. I left corporate America, pivoting in my career path to private security. I spent 15 years protecting tribal leaders from the Mexican cartel. This is analogous to the Secret Service to the President of the United States. I have also protected members of the Royal Family from the Middle East. My work also included managing disaster response teams and managing operations for clients visiting the U.S. President.

My business ventures have taught me that money is just a byproduct of serving your clients well. If you do the right thing, good things always come back to you. I had helped a private security company bring in $10 million in revenues over a three-year period. I see this as the good I did which allowed me to stay at home with my dad when he was terminal with the cancer. After he passed, it took me about a year to recover financially.

I began to rebuild once again in 2019.

And then Covid hit.

I am not the kind of guy who can sit around and do nothing. I launched my very first podcast, "The Fearless Mindset," mid-2019 in honor of my father's fearless mindset during his battle with brain cancer. And it has been the single most rewarding move in my adult life. I would have never dreamed of the guests I have had come onto my show, along with so many business opportunities. The show would not be what it is today without the support of so many amazingly talented men and women. I must give credit where credit is due.

As the host of "The Fearless Mindset" podcast, I have observed that my high-powered guests have several things in common. They are very successful in their tradecraft. They are very busy people. They don't spend much time on social media nor do they watch much news. They are simply too busy mastering their day. They don't allow a minute to be wasted. They have very structured routines. There are such distinct differences between the W2-Mindset and the Owner-Mindset. They think differently. Imagine how fearless Tom Brady had to be in his mindset to now own the most Super Bowl titles. Likewise, Michael Jordon had to own that same fearless mindset to win six NBA titles.

Losing my dad to brain cancer has given me eyes into this next chapter of my life. The gift he left me inspired me to become an inspiration to others. How would you respond if the doctor told you had six more months to live? What actions would you take? What relationships would you forgive and, perhaps, work on re-establishing? You have nothing to lose. What business ventures would you entertain? What is on your bucket list?

Dad taught me to live each day as if it were my last! This is what has driven me to become fearless in business. I have nothing to lose but fear itself.

CHAPTER NINETEEN

~

Follow Your Creative Heart

by Mary Elizabeth Jackson
Owner, J5 Edutainment Inc
www.MaryEJackson.com

The entrepreneurial journey today is vastly different than it was. We have more options and opportunities available to us to succeed as an entrepreneur than ever before. Social media has now become an entrepreneur's way of climbing the corporate ladder. Instead of impressing the boss with your new idea, creation, or product, you need to impress the world. The web is where we give our "60-second elevator speech." It has become our calling card.

I had no idea when I was younger I would be an entrepreneur except that I loved making and creating things that made others happy. When I was a child, I would sit and watch my papa spend hours putting beads on a string and sell them to the ladies in the retirement park where he and my granny lived. They would hang in the window so anyone interested could come by and pick out what they wanted. He was an inventor with an eighth-grade education. He created the first dumpster but was never given credit for the invention. Which unfortunately happened in business more back then. That dumpster he invented is the one that we have today that's used everywhere.

I did not realize how watching him would affect and inspire me. In high school, I made earrings for my girlfriends and fellow dance corps members. They were tiny bows the color of our team, and I glued them onto tiny little earring posts. I continued to make them in my early twenties when I worked at a theme park in Orlando, Florida. I was self-taught and had an internal drive to do this but no understanding of where the drive came from. This inner drive has been the case in my life over and over again.

I did not start the entrepreneurial journey again till I was in my thirties. When my oldest daughter was nine months old, I started a candy business out of my home. I had no real idea what I was doing, no one to guide me, no training, just a drive to do something and succeed. Again, I was self-taught. I loved being creative and making beautiful creations. This can come in endless ways. So I made gourmet candies. I made different flavors, molds, and shapes, and chocolate-dipped cherries. The alcohol-soaked ones were the most popular item I offered. I would buy or create beautiful boxes to put them in. Being on a budget (actually not having one to work with) forces you to be even more creative.

I would get into my car with my nine-month-old daughter and drive up and down the road from town to town where we lived, and I would go into businesses trying to sell my candies. I named the business "Elissa's Treasures" after my daughter. For a one-woman show at the time, they became trendy for a while. My husband would come home, and there would be ticket orders taped all over the kitchen cabinets and boxes or baskets everywhere. He would shake his head and say, "so how long is it going to last?" He was supportive but thought I was crazy, or maybe this was some post-partum thing. Again, the drive was in me to sell, sell, sell. Do something, have something that was mine. At this point in my life, being a mother was the most important thing to me. The doctors told me I would never have children, so having my daughter was everything. And yet inside me, I needed an identity of something else. I never understood it back then and struggled with the guilt of "why do I need to do something more?" But I completely understand it now and am grateful that I listened to that part of me that needed to be acknowledged. The part that needed a voice and a channel to express itself. Each of us needs this outlet. It helps to empower us to make ourselves more whole.

After my second daughter was born, I started a jewelry business with a friend. We both had two small children and wanted to do something creative, have a business, and help make other women feel beautiful and empowered. *Silver Moon Jewelry* was born. We did very well for five years. We had designs in stores everywhere in the area we lived and beyond and a lot of private customers. We did all the shows and festivals every year that we could and made many one-of-a-kinds. It was a lot of hard work, and we loved it. Again, I was self-taught, and I could look at a pile of beads, crystals, stones, pearls, silver, and gold pieces and see designs. That was my favorite part, and I could design all day. I would dream about designs and wake up and draw them. I still see some of those designs when I go to shows or am in a jewelry store today. Our business got busier than we could handle as our kiddos got bigger, and our partnership fell apart for financial and personal reasons. I learned one of the business no-nos. Do not go into business with a friend. Make sure your contract is outlined very well that everything is transparent, and you know what is happening with all of the money. Just because you have a friendship doesn't mean being business partners is a good idea.

My entrepreneurial journey continued in my late 40s when I became a published author. This was not something I had ever done before or known would be a part of my life. I had dreamed about being published. My first book was born after my late in life surprise son arrived. My heart and passion were involved in this, and so much has blossomed since then. The first book –*Perfectly Precious Poohlicious*, won The Gold Maxy Literary Award in 2017, three months after it was published, and it's part of a three-book series. The third book, *Poohlicious Oh the Wonder of Me*, was released on June 2, 2021.

I have an eight-book series in progress, a middle-grade reader coming out in September 2021, a children's journal, and an adult motivational book that will come out soon. I took it a step further with an idea for a platform and co-founded and co-host a livestream show for authors with a friend. Three years later and on The Writers Corner Live TV Show, we have done over 133 interviews of authors all over the globe from debut to New York Times bestsellers. Our show airs live on Amazon Live, Facebook, LinkedIn, Twitter, and YouTube. We also share all things about the writing world. I also collaborate with others as well as ghostwrite and am the voice on the Sport2Gether app.

I am an advocate for special needs and disabilities. It is a very big part of my life. I have two children on the autism spectrum. I wanted to do something educational, empowering, and helpful for those with disabilities and their families. So I co-founded and co-host a livestream show called Special Needs TV. It features everything about the special needs world. My son and I do a live video series with our local library doing science experiments and crafts for all kids, whether they have challenges or not. We are working on a YouTube series featuring children's book reviews and sharing tools and items that can be used for kids with challenges and sensory issues. I am using the written word and social media to help empower kids and others.

When you have a dream, love, or passion, you can turn it into something more. Something bigger that can be of service to others. You have to first take a step forward. What are you passionate about? Can it help someone else? What are you an expert in? This is your place to begin. Your building blocks. What makes your heart sing and makes you get out of bed every day? You may have to try a few things out and see what is successful. As you have read, it took me a while to figure out what was my 'thing.' But when I did, the doors opened wide, and I have been able to merge two of my loves in life, and they balance and support each other.

Being an entrepreneur can mean many different things. One of the main ingredients in all of this is not to give up. To always look ahead and keep moving forward. Do not give up on yourself even when you are not sure what you are doing. Read up on successful people and their stories of all they went through to get where they are. Find a successful person doing what you want to do and ask if they will consider mentoring you. I promise you every step you take to move in the direction that you want to go will get you where you want to be. Use your creative abilities and belief in yourself. You cannot fail; it just may take a little time to get there.

CHAPTER TWENTY

~

How I Kicked Fear and Worry Out of the Driver's Seat of My Life

by Missy Holder
Owner, Missy Holder Coaching
www.MissyHolder.com

As I waved to my girls as they rode off on the school bus with my 9-month-old son on my hip, an overwhelming sense of doom rushed over me. The prior weekend we had moved into my parents' home while we awaited the completion of our new home. I quickly brushed it off as my mind and body were exhausted from the activities of the weekend. My husband had not felt well during the move and had taken a rare sick day that sunny Monday in May. Unusual and concerning symptoms developed as his illness progressed each day. He passed out in the shower and had a persistent cough, a temperature of 104.5 and little red dots, which we later learned were petechiae, around his eyes. By Thursday we found ourselves in an oncologist/hematologist's office with an "unusual" blood test result which required additional interpretation and guidance from the hematologist. "Thank goodness we aren't here to see an oncologist," I thought as I looked around at the bald patients awaiting their appointments.

Within minutes of being ushered into the treatment room, the doctor told me I had to leave the room so she could perform a bone marrow biopsy on my husband. She looked at the clock… 2:50 PM. She had ten minutes to perform the biopsy before the labs would be picked up for the day and she said it was urgent his results were sent out immediately. Upon completion of the biopsy, she told me to take him straight to the hospital where they were awaiting his arrival. "Can we go home to pack our bags first?" I asked. "No. Your husband's white blood cell count is so low, I don't want him to die before we even have a diagnosis," she stated bluntly.

Throughout the next day, as Tim slept in the hospital bed, I was inundated with information regarding the "neutropenic" protocol, which is when a patient's white blood cell count, the infection fighters, is dangerously low. I had to wear a mask around him and wash my hands frequently. Our children were not permitted to visit him as they are little petri dishes of germs. He could not be around fresh flowers or put black pepper on his food (not that he was eating at the time). My head was swirling with anxiety as I tried to process the events. What is happening to our life? What is wrong with Tim? How can I fix this? What is God trying to teach me? What did I do wrong? The never-ending tape played over and over in my head.

Despite not yet having a diagnosis, the next morning Tim was transported via ambulance to a hospital that specialized in blood cancers. It was the Friday before Memorial Day, so we were particularly anxious to receive the results of the bone marrow biopsy fearful we would have to wait until Tuesday if we missed this Friday window. At 5:00 PM the doctor walked in the room. I sat on the bed next to Tim as our families gathered around when the doctor spoke. "Tim has acute lymphoblastic leukemia," he stated. He continued to say more about the condition, but my mind could not comprehend his words. I felt disconnected from the experience, as if I were watching the scene of a movie. I recall crying uncontrollably as the doctor left the room.

Within hours of the diagnosis, Tim had a device surgically implanted in his neck. The device had 4 lines that could simultaneously infuse chemo, meds and fluids directly into his body. His treatment program started the next day, which also happened to be my birthday… the worst birthday in my 37 years of life. This began a three-year treatment journey for my husband. It included countless chemo infusions, brain irradiation, spinal taps, bone marrow biopsies and blood transfusions. I watched my husband fight with courage, grace, determination and humility. I witnessed his relationship with God mature as he relied on Him for the strength to get through each day and gave Him all the glory for allowing him to live another day. My husband truly is the closest to a real-life superhero I know, and I am blessed to be his wife. He has been cancer-free for fifteen years and counting and we are forever grateful!

Having gone through this experience, I am a different person. Prior to Tim's cancer journey, I had allowed two emotions to control the driver's seat of my life journey. These unwelcome guests were worry and fear. Worry lured me in to believing I was the one controlling the wheel as we traveled. Fear told me to avoid challenging and uncomfortable paths in my life. Both directed my journey as I wandered without a clear intention or purpose.

Previously I was dubbed "worry wart" by friends and family. I wore this title as a badge of honor convincing myself that my worry was somehow correlated to my level of love and dedication to those about whom I worried. When my husband was gravely ill, the weight of that worry was more than I could bear. I literally could not carry that level of worry as it was too burdensome. It was then I realized I never controlled anything by worrying in the past either. Worrying gave me a feeling of control over my life, a façade that came crashing down with the news of Tim's cancer. Surprisingly, I discovered a new sense of emotional freedom and weightlessness when I no longer carried the burden of worry. Born out of necessity, this newfound practice of not worrying became a part of who I strive to be today. I recognize worry as the thief that it is, as it steals joy from our days. I choose to seek the blessings in all situations, even when life is challenging.

Formerly, I allowed fear to dictate the choices I made with my life. I preferred to play sports in which I felt certain I would excel. I chose a career path in which I felt comfortable. I embraced familiarity over challenge and adventure in nearly all my life's decisions. Fear provided the illusion of serving me well in its attempts to keep me safe emotionally. In reality, it forced me to play small, to not risk failure or accept challenges. As with worry, I began to recognize fear as the thief that it is, as I was allowing it to steal growth opportunities that would allow me to become the best version of myself. I kicked worry and fear out of the driver's seat of my life and replaced them with intention and purpose.

While walking alongside my husband as he literally fought for his life changed who I am; more importantly, the experience transformed my view on life itself. Confronting mortality so intimately and authentically shifted my views on life's meaning and purpose. I resolved that I would no longer wander aimlessly through life without intention. I defined who I was and what values for which I stood and resolved to live in alignment with these. I determined my sole purpose was to care for my husband and to raise my three young children. I was living in alignment with my God-given purpose, and I was fulfilled, joyful and content.

Over the past decade, our two girls have grown into strong, independent, compassionate, beautiful women who graduated college, entered the workforce and are officially adulting. Our soon-to-be sixteen-year-old son is maturing into an independent, kind-hearted, intelligent young man with aspirations of attending college to further his education and pursue his dreams. While the God-given responsibility of motherhood will always be my sole purpose, I am in a season of life in which the role is shifting. This role simply occupies less time, which allowed me the opportunity to reflect and redefine my purpose.

At the age of 51 I launched my entrepreneurial journey as a personal growth coach. I empower women to define their goals, develop an action plan, enlist their support system, equip them to overcome obstacles and evaluate and adjust course as needed. Together we identify which limiting beliefs she has allowed to dictate her life journey. Perhaps her drivers have been fear of failure, fear of rejection, fear of success, perfectionism, or overthinking. I support each woman as she resumes control of the wheel. Most importantly, I encourage her to embrace and enjoy her beautifully messy and imperfect journey of growth. By expecting and welcoming the discomfort associated with taking imperfect action, each woman experiences surprising fulfillment and joy. Like me she will experience fear on her growth journey, but she will no longer allow it to dictate her path. True courage is not the absence of fear; rather feeling the fear and doing it anyway. Be courageous and live your best life!

CHAPTER TWENTY-ONE

~

Step Up and Speak Out

by Mistie Layne
Founder, Write 2 Ignite Women's
Empowerment Retreats
www.StepUpAndSpeakOut.com

How many times have you allowed FEAR to keep you from being your true authentic self? How many ideas/dreams have you had and never taken action to achieve? Many desire entrepreneurship for the money, making our own hours, achieving our dreams, etc. However, being a fearless entrepreneur comes from a place of passion for me because I truly feel led to Step Up and Speak Out about the adversity I have overcome in order to overcome my worst and live my best in an attempt to help inspire others to pull themselves up!

My journey has been a long one that has deemed me an Empowerment and Resiliency expert due to the "overcoming" I have endured. I went from being on the brink of becoming a surgeon to facing a forty-year prison sentence behind a horrific cocaine addiction. Left vulnerable, depressed and searching for validation after a divorce, I tried cocaine for the first time at age 32, a mother of two in medical school that should have known better. I didn't respect my moment of choice and that addiction led me through a decade of domestic abuse, rape, assault, prostitution, abortions, and many other countless harmful situations I could have died from. While doing the wrong things in the wrong places with the wrong people, I was attacked and lost control of my car, and killed somebody that dreadful day September 18th. I served time in prison and faced fears daily such as; death threats, rape, being isolated from my kids, and fearing I didn't deserve to live (Survivor's Guilt).

Writing my life story in prison became the therapy that saved my life. I learned to find gratitude for what I had (even in a tiny jail cell) instead of focusing on what I didn't. I wrote my pain away and confronted my fears of judgment, forgiveness and rehabilitation. I put the work in and dealt with the pain, one thing at a time by seeking counseling, asking forgiveness from others, learning to forgive other people, and, most importantly, discovering how to forgive myself. Once released from prison, I didn't release my now bestselling book, *What Goes Up*, because I feared judgment. Instead, I sat on it, hiding my past and allowing all secrets to boil like toxic acid in my body. It wasn't until after my grandbaby (born on the same day of the wreck 8 years prior) was born with a severe brain injury that left her blind, deaf, speechless, and so many others problems, that I realized I was letting my past rob my future. I blamed myself for her birth injury because the dates couldn't have been a coincidence, right? I decided her condition was my punishment! I then realized I was now a survivor, an authority if you will, on addiction, domestic abuse, abortion grief, rape issues, and many other things I had survived. I decided it was time to STEP UP AND SPEAK OUT with transparency in order to help ease suffering of others. My past no longer held me hostage with secrets, lies and fear of judgment.

My passion to be an entrepreneur running my Write 2 Ignite Women's Empowerment Retreats and my e360 tv talk show, Dare 2 Share with Mistie Layne, is driven by desire to help others. I am fearless when it comes to spreading inspirational story after story because I feel they educate us to JUDGE less and MENTOR more. I coach others as an Empowerment and Resiliency expert to transform their lives by releasing toxic beliefs through transparency to overcome any adversity with confidence and resiliency.

Anything worth having requires tenacity, diligence, and courage to face those fears to accomplish the task. If it were easy, everybody would be an entrepreneur, but ask yourself what is driving you to take that bold step. Once you have identified WHY you are doing it, focus on that and let that be your powering force to succeed.

Instead of letting one roadblock after another get in my way, I tackle them head on by reminding myself of my WHY. Utilize these steps to become a FEARLESS ENTREPRENEUR:

1. When FEAR hits and you feel stressed with sweaty palms and a rapid heartbeat, recognize this is your body actually giving you the increased strength to power through it. USE IT to propel forward.

2. The only part of FEAR you control is your response to it! Find the pieces you can conquer and take action...

3. Confront the FEAR by devising a plan to minimize the stress. Break it down into small pieces and deal with one component at a time. Accept what you can control, and surrender to what you can't, then adapt. Find what works for you and practice it over and over.

4. Reframe your mindset and value what is waiting on you on the other side of your FEAR. Think of fear as the top of a mountain; once you get there, it's all downhill. Be careful not to let the mountain (FEAR) itself prevent you from taking that action to tackle it.

5. Find the meaning and lessons in FEAR itself. What will you gain from confronting it and how can you use that energy to propel you forward and also help others? Don't succumb to the stress of fear, take action to defeat it and achieve your goals.

Life happens to all of us, and we will face bumps in the road ahead, but we must remember our WHY and use our resources to stand apart. I am facing roadblocks and challenges right now, but I choose to power through and tackle each situation as it comes, determined to conquer with resiliency. We lost my granddaughter, Eliana, in 2020 and watching my daughter hold her daughter as she took her last breath was unimaginable pain, but we got through it by communicating, understanding that grief plays an important role in healing, and by facing it head on. Additionally, my life has been turned upside down with my mom being diagnosed with cancer and living with me because her house was hit by two hurricanes back-to-back. A tree fell through the roof of my daughter's house during one of those hurricanes, while we were in it! My daughter was 7 months pregnant at the time and we just powered through, moving them out of their house and figuring it out one day at a time as we rebuild. Freak ice storms have hit us, medical issues, surgeries, etc.... because LIFE HAPPENS. I believe what we do as a person on the OTHER SIDE OF ADVERSITY is what sets us apart.

CHAPTER TWENTY-TWO

Note to Self

by Monica Allen
Co-Owner, Zeus' Closet & stuff4GREEKS
www.StitchedForSuccess.com

In the warmth of my small three-bedroom, one-bath home where I grew up, the ringing of our black, rotary wall-mounted telephone blared through the quiet of a cold winter day. I heard my mom answer and say, "I have not seen him. No, I have not heard from him." She got off the phone and explained to my then-5-year-old self that my paternal grandmother was looking for my dad. We would find out a couple of days later that he was safe, but had hopped on a Greyhound bus headed to New Jersey, leaving our small southern town behind and leaving me, his only child, behind as well. I would go on to see my biological father three times from the day he left until the time he died when I was 17.

I would grow up in a very loving home with my grandmother, mother and uncle, but the older I got, the more I realized that we were poor. My mom had me at the age of 18. There were not a lot of opportunities for people with a college degree, let alone people without a degree, to have a meaningful and lucrative career in our small town. I can honestly say, though, that I was never hungry and I was never cold or homeless, but there were not a lot of name brand fashions or extracurricular activities for this little girl, and I was often embarrassed to be on free and reduced lunch. My mom stayed at home with me until around the time my dad left town. She went to work alongside my grandmother at the local sewing factory. I can remember that she absolutely hated that job. Years later she became a preschool teacher, making less than $700 per month, but at least she had a passion for that position.

I knew early on that I wanted a different life. I knew that I did not want to have kids at a young age because I knew that I wanted to have more opportunities. My grandmother often said to me," Baby, you make sure you go to school and get a good education." I cannot even begin to count how many times I heard that as a child and teenager. My grandmother had only gone through sixth grade and had to leave school to go work on the family farm. She was never able to return to school and she had her first child in her teens as well. I had to break the cycle so I followed my grandmother's instruction, graduating from high school with honors, and heading off to college to be the first person in my immediate family to graduate from a four-year institution and go on to get my Master's degree.

When asked to be a part of this book, I took a moment to think about what makes me fearless. Truth be told, I am not always fearless, but I can reflect on elements of my life that continue to propel me forward and make me never give up on my goals, dreams, and the vision I have for my life and those of future generations. I want to share those things with you. I like to call them my *"Note to Self"* moments.

My mindset is propelled by my history.
— **Monica Allen @StitchedForSuccess**

My maternal grandfather, whom I never met, was considered a successful and wealthy entrepreneur in the rural south. He owned a corner store, property and livestock. When he suddenly passed away in his 40s, his mother tricked his children out of their inheritance. She had my grandmother, who was illiterate, sign documents giving up all of their rights to his property. His mother was half white and had much more power with the lawyers in our town than my grandmother. Unfortunately, like many people, he did not have a will to ensure that his children would be cared for should something happen to him. He passed just a few months prior to my birth, and after hearing this story for many years while growing up, I knew two things. One: I had entrepreneurship running through my veins. And two:

> *Note to Self*: Nothing like this would ever happen to me. I will read every contract thoroughly and make sure my kids can read practically as soon as they come out of the womb.
>
> *My 2nd grade teacher buried the word 'can't.'*
> — **Monica Allen @StitchedForSuccess**

I remember the first day of second grade almost like it was yesterday. I can almost literally transport myself back to the classroom. I can feel the light in the class and remember exactly where I was sitting when my second grade teacher walked up to the green chalkboard, drew a lumpy, white chalk line on the board and wrote the word "can't" underneath the line. She told us that the word "can't" was buried in our classroom and that we were not allowed to use it. That has stuck with me for over 30 years. I now even tell my kids this. When I have a thought that enters my mind even close to "I can't do something," it is immediately pushed away because I remember Mrs. Wynn's statement all those years ago. When I wanted to study abroad and knew that I could not afford it, for example, I did not give up. I did not say, "I can't do this because I don't have the money." I figured out how to get the money. When I want to do something bad enough, I will find a way. "Can't" is buried.

> *Note to Self:* "Can't" does not exist. It has been buried and I can always accomplish and do anything I truly desire.

Another pivotal moment in my life was learning to set and write down my goals. When I was a college student and decided to apply to be a resident assistant, I landed the position after a number of interviews. The first thing our boss had us do was write down 5-7 goals that we had for the year. I have always had things in my mind that I wanted to accomplish, but this was the first time I had ever written them down. After writing them down and taking them to our next staff meeting, he said "Great! I will keep one copy and you put the other one up in your room. Do not bury them in your desk, but put them on your bulletin board or somewhere you can see them." I followed his instructions. The paper did eventually get buried on my corkboard by many other things so I did not look at my goals every day, but at the end of the year when I was emptying my room and clearing the bulletin board, I noticed that I had accomplished every goal that I had written on my list! From that point on, I truly believed in the power of writing down goals and envisioning what I want to accomplish.

> *Note to Self:* Goals are key to accomplishing everything. Goals invoke vision and once you can see it, you can be it and do it.

Go foR IT each and every day.
— **Monica Allen @StitchedForSuccess**

My grandmother had tenacity, hustle and, most of all, grit unlike anyone I have ever met. In addition to working in a sewing plant as a bundle girl, she cleaned homes and cooked meals to make ends meet. Her kids were never hungry and always had a roof over their head. She raised three kids as a black, single mom buying her own home and cars in the Jim Crow south. My grandmother worked hard her entire life.

> *Note to Self:* I have no excuses. I have opportunities that my grandmother could only *dream* of or wish for in her life.

When I first entered corporate America, I was excited. I was excited to have reached what I thought was the pinnacle of that "good job" my grandmother spoke of and being in a high rise office building in Buckhead, a ritzy area in Midtown Atlanta...surely I had made it. I was excited to learn new skills and to use my degree that I worked hard for and went into debt to earn. I was on my way to bigger and better things. However, after about 5 years, corporate America had lost its lustre. I began to get the inklings of my entrepreneurial spirit bubbling up. Then one day I got a sign that it was time to move forward on my own dreams and vision. When I entered the elevator at the corporate office, our local manager of the global insurance brokerage I worked for was in there as well. As I arrived at my floor, I stepped off of the elevator and he continued on up to his office, an office that I knew I would never reach. The glass ceiling was real and at that moment I knew that if I wanted to be in charge, it would have to be of my own making.

Note to Self: I will create my own floor and ceiling because I will own my own company. I will own the entire building and determine my own income.

As I took the leap and began my own business, these are many of the lessons throughout life that have helped me to press on. Press on when loans were denied. Press on when we faced a lawsuit. Press on when three essential team members left abruptly after I had just had our first baby. Press on when an expensive piece of equipment was stolen in the middle of the night. Press on when payroll could barely be met. Press on when an employee leaked trade secrets to a competitor. Press on even when a pandemic happens. Press on and be fearless no matter what comes my way.

CHAPTER TWENTY-THREE

~

What's Your Plan, God?

by Sally Green
Founder, The Self-Care Rockstar
www.TheSelfcareRockstar.com

My Why ...

When I was 18 months old, I reached up and grabbed a boiling pot of water off the stove. I was burned from my armpit to my feet. While in the hospital, I developed a staph infection and was in a coma for three days. The doctors told my parents there was little hope I would survive. My grandmother and aunts had members of their churches praying round the clock. Of course I don't remember any of this, but these stories have been told to me as long as I can remember.

My grandfather used to tell me that when they said I was too sick for visitors, and he had to beat up the doctor in order to see me. That story always made me laugh as a child.

As a teen, I would often ask God why he had not taken me when he could have. I came to the conclusion that God must have something for me to do. My life has become a search for that meaning, often taking jaunts in the wrong direction.

Selling Makeup

After high school, I desperately wanted to go to college, but no one in my family had college degrees or business experience. Besides, there was no money for college. I was working full time in a machine shop and they had a tuition reimbursement program. I applied for it and was accepted. I began taking college classes at night while working full time. It took me six years to get my two-year Associates Degree in Computer Science.

One of the women I met in college invited me to a makeup party. It was called Aloette Cosmetics and I loved the products. This was in the mid '80s and home shows were a big business. I was offered the opportunity to sell them and soon became one of the top salespeople in Connecticut. I loved meeting new people, applying makeup, and selling. I was good at selling, but not good at recruiting others. I sold makeup part time for eight years until right before my daughter was born in 1994. I thought that maybe I was meant to help women look beautiful? I was still trying to figure out why I was spared.

Housecleaning Plus

When my daughter was born, I was working for a computer service company. I loved the job, but it became cheaper for businesses to purchase new computers than to service old ones. Right after I returned from maternity leave, I was laid off. I collected unemployment for a while, but needed to find a better source of income.

My cousin told me about a friend who was looking for a house cleaning service. I contacted her friend and began cleaning houses. I started with two accounts and soon it grew to five days a week with a waiting list. My clients were parents with children, elderly, and the disabled. In addition to cleaning, I helped with a variety of other tasks including caring for pets, driving to appointments, and helping with computer issues, etc. My business became a ministry of sorts and many of my customers became good friends.

Spiritual Growth

In 2006, as my daughter was about to enter middle school, a customer mentioned to me that there was a group in town praying for a teen Bible study. I got really excited. That night I couldn't sleep thinking about how wonderful a group Bible study would be for my daughter. I had been a Sunday school teacher at that point for almost 20 years and was thinking about all the lessons I could teach.

The next morning my phone rang. Believing it to be my mother, I did not look at the caller ID and answered it. It was Debbie from the prayer group. My customer had given her my phone number because I had been so excited about it when we talked.

Debbie and I started a teen Bible study with the six middle school students from our two churches. Three years later, we had over 50 students regularly attending our weekly Bible study; it was an amazing experience. I grew so much spiritually during that time.

After the teen Bible study ended, I took a lay speaking course. I felt that God wanted me to use my voice. I began leading worship at church when our minister would go on vacation or was sick. I felt God was preparing me for a future endeavor, and I was right.

Expanding the Cleaning Business

My husband was working in sales at a sunroom construction company in 2008 when the housing market crashed. He lost his job. I was doing well in the cleaning business and he had often come to help me on weekends and days off. We decided he would join full time and we would add rug cleaning and window washing to the service. We increased our residential customers and began looking for commercial accounts.

We were offered a commercial account on weekday mornings. With that account, our increased residential customers and special jobs, we were able to make ends meet.

I always wanted more, though. I was getting tired of cleaning other people's dirt. We had been cleaning for so long and it was what I knew how to do. I had no idea how to do something else. I worked harder and longer hours than I ever had before. I became complacent and just didn't care. Over the years I had gained more than 80 pounds, I was ashamed to tell people what I did for a living and, although I was never formally diagnosed, I knew I was suffering from depression. I was happy on the outside but felt dejected and like a loser on the inside.

Family Issues

In 2017 my father had a massive heart attack. He was in a medically induced coma for three months. My mom was a wreck. She had always been a worrier and we began to notice she was having trouble remembering things. After dad came home, mom's memory problems became more apparent. At the end of 2019 my mom was diagnosed with Alzheimer's. It's been an uphill battle and so emotional at times watching someone I love suffering from this dreadful disease.

Art had been the one thing that grounded me. I loved painting and was taking some online classes. I decided I would start my own paint and sip business and in January of 2020 I began making plans to teach. I contacted a few senior living facilities and started teaching monthly classes in February. My church allowed me to use the facility for my Saturday morning coffee and canvas classes. I even secured a large fundraiser for a local cat rescue program. Then Covid hit and it was all cancelled.

After Covid hit and we were in lockdown, our commercial cleaning account decided they wanted to go in a different direction. They contacted us to say they were not renewing our contract. It felt like every time I hit rock bottom someone else would throw me shovel and say, "keep digging." One thing I always had was my sense of humor and the ability to pivot.

The Transformation

With everything I was facing, my mom's illness, losing a big portion of our income by losing the commercial account, my art business on hold, I looked in the mirror one morning and didn't recognize the person looking back. How could I have let myself get so overweight? How could my life be so out of control? I knew I wasn't the only one going through difficulties, but my life was the only one I could change. So, I made a decision that day. I was going to get healthier; I was going to learn how to run a business better, and I was going to come out of Covid a lean, mean, fighting machine.

I started walking regularly with my daughter and husband. We researched healthy meals we would enjoy and started cooking them. I stopped watching tv news, started reading self-help books, and took up journaling again. I signed up for Cardone University and began meditating in the mornings.

Changing all those small habits little by little over a matter of months began to add up to big changes. I lost 40 pounds, had more energy, felt better than I had in years. I was offered the opportunity to be a contributing author in a book with Forbes Riley and Les Brown and jumped at the chance. I soon became a 2-time international bestselling author. I joined a mastermind with Lynda Sunshine West and started another new business called, "The Self-Care Rockstar," I am speaking and teaching the self-care habits and lessons I learned over the past 16 months.

My search for why God allowed me to live all those years ago has created in me a fearless attitude to take action. I am excited to see where this new business takes me. Will this be the home run that catapults me into living my life's purpose? or will it be just another steppingstone in that direction? Stay tuned…

CHAPTER TWENTY-FOUR

Faith Over Fear

by Shanna Lee Moore
Owner, Developing True Health &
Justice Massage
www.DevelopingTrueHealth.com

What comes to mind when you hear the word FEAR? Some say, "False Evidence Appearing Real." For others it's "Face Everything and Recover." My favorite is "Feeling Excited And Ready!" We will all have things come up from time to time that challenge us. Bob Proctor says, "If a goal doesn't scare you a little, it's not big enough!" Goals are designed to help us grow.

I remember growing up and having all kinds of dreams and fantasies. I was curious, creative and caring. From having an imaginary friend to trying to adopt a horse at age 7, I was always dancing to the beat of a different drum. Childhood instability and unmet dreams stifled that inner warrior. My little girl was "locked in the closet" to be protected from the uncertainty and chaos. She stayed there for many years until I was finally ready to face my past and heal. I would find forgiveness in my heart for the people, places and things that stood in the way of my visions. This included giving grace to the well-intentioned counselor that said photography was a "hobby and not a career" even though I placed 1st and 3rd in the Del Mar Fair in High School. My forgiveness extended to my past choices that caused all my early poetry to be "lost." I would come to terms with the neighborhoods where I "lived" when I was homeless. I became an entrepreneur for every dream I have put on hold and to give my kids the best life possible.

I always wanted my kids to have a better life than I did. "Better" is a very subjective word. I wanted them to have more than I had. More choices and more opportunities. I wanted their voices to be heard and for them to never feel discouraged from following their dreams.

When I was a single mom with my oldest daughter, Justice, I had the choice to either get a job or go back to school. Knowing that fast food and customer service weren't going to provide the lifestyle I wanted for us, I chose school to become a certified massage therapist. I was told up front that due to some of the wreckage of my past, I may have a challenge getting my license. I didn't let that deter me. I enrolled and took the necessary steps to clean up my past mistakes. I had always had a natural ability to massage and relieve pain by finding people's knots. Now it was my job. I worked at a pain relief center and had private clients to earn extra money for fun things with my daughter.

One day I was promoting my boss' company and met a woman who would change my life. She saw something in me that I had buried long ago. She taught me about the cash flow quadrants and leveraged income. She asked me a very important question: "At the end of the month, after travel to work and living expenses, how much money do you have left?" Since I was receiving government assistance, the answer was "none." Even though basic needs were met, I wasn't making it on my own. I needed something else. My income was limited to how many massages I was physically able to perform in 24 hours.

She shared her business with me, which was a home-based business where money could be made through referrals from anywhere I had my phone. I prayed about the opportunity. My prayers were answered when the needed start-up funds became available. My health changed! I didn't even realize I was unhealthy. My mind changed! I started reading great books and surrounding myself with positive people. I wanted to share with everyone I cared about. I wanted them to know their dreams could come true, too. I really just wanted to help. Some heard me out, some didn't believe me and some completely cut me from their life. For a while I was frustrated. They clearly saw what happened for me. I even offered free samples and yet they didn't accept. I had to come to terms that some people aren't ready or willing to change their situation.

We have paradigms that control our behavior. These can be rooted more deeply than we realize. I'm still working on uncovering and rewriting mine, including getting over my fears of rejection, self-doubt, and lack of confidence. At first I thought I needed to imitate everything about my mentor to achieve success. I was too dependent. I didn't master the skills needed to step into my role as a leader. So, I distanced myself. Taking a step back gave me clarity and allowed me to discover myself again. Who am I and what do I really want? I worked from a perspective of improving my weaker points and enhancing my strengths. I challenged myself to find alignment with my purpose and take action steps every day to achieve my goals.

Success is never a straight line. The ups and downs make the journey interesting. The year 2020 was eye opening. Some of my shadows came out. I was unable to see massage clients. I had my other business, but I was so depressed from the external situation that I didn't call or share with anyone. I embraced my new role as a homeschool teacher and stay-at-home wife. (Domestic duties have never been my strong suit.) During this time, I connected with another wonderful mentor.

I started listening to positive audios and getting back into association with dreamers and doers. I now had more to share with my kids. The more they learn earlier in life, the better their chances will be.

Unparalleled educational information for all the important areas of our lives is readily available. I shared this information with some, but then blocks arose again: the fear of the unknown, the fear of change, and maybe even the fear of success, or feeling unworthy stopped me from taking action. I then entered a manifestation portal. I was surrounded by love and light by both women and men who had their own dreams and who held strong, positive visions for mine coming to fruition. The daily support and love felt through our connection is so powerful. So many of the things being spoken into the space were catapulted into the physical world. I am becoming a manifestor.

It's amazing the power felt by completely encouraging yourself and others that ANYTHING is possible! Even writing this chapter is a step toward one of my dreams (to be an author and published poet). So, thank you! Thank you for being here to witness this transformation. Thank you for believing in yourself and your dreams. Thank you for saying YES to opportunities. Thank you for your creativity, courage and collaboration. I'll leave you with one of my poems:

Fear may come and fear will go.
Some of its causes you may not know.
It's valid to experience at times.
Mostly it all comes from within our minds.

The voice inside that says we can't,
It goes on and on like a rant.
There is another voice in there too.
It's usually much quieter when it speaks to you.

The voice of desires and dreams.
Can you hear it over the screams?
Listen closely to your heart.
It knows the way; it's very smart.

The path to what you really desire,
The passion inside you that burns like fire.
Keep adding kindling and fan with air,
Keep envisioning with lots of flare.

Whatever you see in your mind and hold in your heart.
It will be yours, you just need to start.
Start today to take an action or two.
You can reach all your dreams, it's up to you.
Don't let fears hold you back,
Make a plan and then attack!

There are many people in this world who want you to succeed. They are more than happy to share ideas and inspiration with you. I know because I am one of them! Please reach out to me if there is anything I can help you with. This life is a gift. It is a beautiful creation that we are blessed to experience. Never make a permanent decision based on a temporary situation. You can have anything you put your mind to. Sending you love, light, and blessings.

CHAPTER TWENTY-FIVE

~

"I got a REAL job!"

by Sherri Leopold
Founder/CEO, Dream BIG with Sherri Leopold
www.SherriLeopold.com

While teaching preschool in the early fall of 1997, one of the moms came in to pick up her son and she said, "Hey, I am having a party for my sister, and here is a catalog if you want to look at it." I said okay. After looking at it for a while, I was very intrigued. I was also a bit apprehensive. I had never been in business for myself before.

I asked the mom about the company and she directed me to her sister. I had never been part of any direct selling or network marketing company of any kind. I had always worked the typical hourly pay type of job. I was only working part time because I wanted to be able to spend time with my three children who were four, six, and nine years old at the time. Budget constraints were a huge concern with me only working part time. I understood I could develop this kind of business in the evening when my husband was home with the kids. I am a very social person anyway, so this seemed like a fun opportunity.

Without overthinking it, I jumped in with both feet and took off. I even outlasted the person who brought me into the company. She left, and I began to earn trips around the world. I never dreamed I'd be on this journey. I was a college graduate and hadn't ever really considered working for myself in any capacity ever. I envisioned working for some company or social service agency for 40 years and retiring. God had different plans for me.

From the start, I began to get the same question, "Is this a pyramid scheme?" I had to look up the definition so that I understood what I was being asked. For clarification purposes, the Oxford Dictionary states:

> Pyramid Scheme is a form of investment (illegal in the US and elsewhere) in which each paying participant recruits two further participants, with returns being given to early participants using money contributed by later ones.

Whew! That was a relief. I knew I was selling them an actual product they chose, paid for, and received quite happily. Navigating around other people's misconception about this proved much harder, however. I would talk with someone about the business, and their spouse was sure it was a scam of some sort. Sometimes, the harder I worked to help them understand, the more resistant they were. When I earned my first trip in 1998, the negative responses became less. I was living proof that people COULD make money, they COULD earn these trips, and it was a REAL job. I put blinders on and pushed forward!

I have always felt that your work should be aligned with your passion. I got a degree in social services because I aimed to help people. I had no idea that this is HOW I would be helping them. However, it is what my life has always been about. I have always been the perpetual cheerleader. When your professional life is in alignment with your passions, your work doesn't feel like work in the traditional sense. I love people.

Ever since my first network marketing job in 1997, I show up with enthusiasm, joy, and an intention to serve my team and customers. I have always chosen companies where I felt I could serve people with both the product and the income opportunity. Even with the belief that my "sales" job was real, and that it was a viable way to earn a living, I still continued to get the question, "But what do you do full time?"

Ignoring the doubters, I kept moving, building, growing, and learning. In my head, I knew if I stayed focused on building my own dreams, staying in action, people would have to understand at some point. I continued to grow and was still growing, when suddenly, the over 100,000 people who were active in the company all got the same email, "We are sorry to inform you that we have closed." After 31 years in business, they were closing. I was devastated. After earning trips to Hawaii, England, and Switzerland, it was over. Some part of me didn't want to be part of another company, ever. However, a bigger part of me wanted to be part of another team.

One thing I was sure of… I didn't want to return to a full-time nine-to-five job. I moved to another home décor company that was family owned. After one and a half years, and another trip earned to Jamaica, the company attempted to expand after 30 years, and sold to a group of partners. This proved to be fatal, and they too went out of business. Was a dark cloud following me?

I wasn't ready to give up. I researched my network marketing options, and in 2004 I joined another company. Along came 2007, and as I was very close to hitting my first car bonus rank, the bottom dropped out of my business. The products were a higher end skin care system that was hit hard in the 2008 recession. My sales decreased significantly. The company, as a result, also went through some changes, and I realized I needed to step away. I did work for the public school system for quite a while, and I added some different companies here and there, even earning a cruise with a jewelry company.

As the recession was easing, it became easier to research options for companies. The internet was booming and the web evolved into a true super highway of information and it became easier to connect with others. Social Media began to emerge as a tool for both building opportunities AND for ridicule of entrepreneurs. It was easier to connect with people, but also easier for people to make fun, organize groups of haters, and the like. I couldn't believe there were groups created specifically to bash people who cold message them. I simply do not operate in a space where people take time to hate someone's occupation or company. I don't ridicule or mock others for their choice of jobs to support their families. I saw so much of this in the process of growing my teams. I watched many people with great skill sets struggle, not because of a lack of skill, but from a lack of support and self-confidence.

Another big hurdle I have overcome, aside from people not recognizing it as a real job, has been when I have changed companies multiple times. One conversation sticks out. My friend heard me talking, and in her New York accent said, "Whattaya doing NOW?!" I told her my new company, the one I am currently with, and she said, "it's hard for me to keep up!" I was flaming mad. I had a right to work with whatever company I wanted to that made me happy. I thought for a split second, and said, "I want to ask you something. If I sold State Farm insurance for 2 years, and I move over to Country Financial, would you have asked me that same question?" She said, "No, probably not." I asked why. She said, "Because it's insurance," and continued on by saying, "But you have done jewelry, makeup, and now vitamins!" I said, "No, I have done SALES, which just so happened to be with those product lines. My job has not ever changed in the 7 years you have known me! The product has changed, yes, but never my job!" She said,

"Wow! I guess that's right!" She simply didn't understand what my job was. I could have done sales at a car lot, in an insurance agency, or many different settings.

I <u>CHOSE </u>Network Marketing! Almost exclusively because of my boss! She is literally the best boss you could ever have. She lets me work from home, the beach, next to a mountain stream on a hike, or even take the day or week off and still get paid. That boss is ME! That's right. I chose ME over anyone else I could work for! I celebrated my 23rd year anniversary in direct sales/NWM in September of 2020. I am just about to earn my 24th trip in network marketing (to Las Vegas!).

Yes, there are still those who think it isn't a "real" job. Those people do not pay my bills or support my family. They DO see me earning a paycheck, growing a team, and earning trips. If you show up with determination, positive energy, it will deflect any negativity or disbelief anyone puts in your path.

As Yoda says, "There is no try, only DO or do not!" I choose to DO, in a way that brings me joy and fulfillment, and a good paycheck.

I am fearless with action—Do the do, to get the get. Most of all, Choose YOU and DO what makes you happy!

CHAPTER TWENTY-SIX

~

Fear | F.E.A.R. | Fear Less | Fearless

by Tanisha Coffey
Founder, The Lofty Entrepreneur
www.TheLoftyEntrepreneur.com

I have a confession to make. Becoming an entrepreneur was *not* my dream. It wasn't something that I had ever even thought about doing. In fact, I didn't choose entrepreneurship...at least, not willingly. But, as my life unfolds, it's turning out to be the best decision that I never intended to make. Hi! I'm Tanisha Coffey, AKA The Lofty Entrepreneur and this is my story...

Picture it. It's March 2005. I'm a young woman in Atlanta, Georgia, just finishing up my first post-graduate program, earning my certificate in Advertising Copywriting from one of the top schools in the nation. Of the six copywriters admitted to the program in my cohort, I and one other copywriter are the only copywriters who made it through to the eighth quarter. We are among the "elite" and *they* are telling us that we will be among the most hirable copywriters--not just in town, but in the nation.

Call it naivete. Call it wishful thinking. Call it whatever you want, but I believed them.

Admittedly, I wasn't like most of the other grads who were willing to go wherever the job was. Six months prior, I had met a man and I was madly in love with him. So, I didn't want to leave Atlanta. Plus, I actually liked it there. It was the first place I had lived as an adult where I could see myself building a life. So, I wasn't looking for work outside of the metro area...but, I also didn't think I needed to. There were three Goliath advertising agencies in town, lots of major corporations with in-house marketing departments and several local boutique advertising and design firms that had in-house writing teams. Plus, my teachers had worked at or with many of the firms in town. So, I had strong connections and great recommendations.

I know what you're thinking: "You're a shoo-in to get hired!"

I know, right!??!? That's what I thought, too. I had done everything right. Undergrad degree. Post-grad training from a top school. Stellar portfolio. Glowing recommendations from industry professionals. Plus, I had made powerful connections and was tapping into their network.

I *thought* I had thought of everything. I *thought* I had the perfect plan.

In a perfect local economy, that probably would have been enough. But no plan, no thing, is ever perfect. (*Remember that. As an entrepreneur, you're going to need it!*) What I hadn't considered was the greater outside influences that I had zero ability to control.

Unfortunately, I wasn't entering a perfect local economy for my industry. Just as I was preparing to graduate, the advertising industry was in the midst of a huge shake up. Two of the major advertising agencies were merging and the third was firing, not hiring. The result: There were a lot of experienced advertising folks in town who were suddenly out of a job or who found themselves having to take jobs below their experience, just to keep a job. A great portfolio and recommendations don't beat experience. So, I wasn't the creme de la creme candidate anymore.

I spent the next three months applying and applying and applying, trying to get a job. I was on MonsterJobs.com and AJCJobs.com every day, all day, submitting application after application, customizing cover letters and resumes, doing all I knew to do to get a job. I got a few interviews but no job offers. I was growing desperate and despair was setting in.

At that time, I was living on my own and I was relying on the last of my student loan money to pay the bills and eat. I wasn't living the fun life you think most are living in their 20s. I was stressed! I had no income. I had no job offers. Money was running out. And, the last thing I wanted was to have to leave Atlanta...and the guy...to move back home with my mother.

I was terrified of what would happen next. None of what I was going through was part of "the plan." So, there was no plan on how to deal with it. And the optics of it all! How was that going to look? Me, the daughter of two teachers, educated and unemployed, having to go back home to live with my mother. That's not how things were supposed to go. I was *supposed* to be successful like my sister, all of her friends and all my friends had been because I, like them, had followed the rules. I had done EVERYTHING I was told to do to be successful. But, I wasn't.

My fears continued to grow. I was scared of what people would think. I was scared of losing my relationship if I had to leave the state. I was scared of never being able to take care of myself and always having to rely on someone else. That's not how I was raised. I was raised to think and be an independent woman who could take care of herself... but I wasn't and I questioned whether I ever would be.

You're a failure. You must have done something wrong. This is your fault.

Those words played over and over like a CD on repeat in my mind and as each day passed, I felt worse and worse about myself. But, somewhere in there, something clicked. I realized that I could continue pitying myself and that I could keep applying for jobs even though that wasn't getting me the results I was needing. Or, I could try something different; something that was not the prescribed plan, something that was not the touted path to success. I was terrified at the thought of it. I didn't want to be judged--not for making the decision to stop applying and not for not being able to land a job. I felt ashamed.

But, at the end of the day, after processing what was at stake and what would happen if I failed, I came to a realization.

I can keep doing the same thing and continue to have the same result but that'd be crazy, right? Right. And I have nothing to lose...literally. I've been doing what I was told and I still don't have a job. Worst case scenario, I stay in the same boat with no income and I have to move home. So, if no one will hire me, maybe I should hire myself!

And that's how life shoved me into entrepreneurship.

My path from there continued to be filled with challenges. My fears didn't go away overnight and I didn't suddenly become a fearless entrepreneur. After all, I was in completely uncharted territory! I didn't have anyone to mentor me as a freelance copywriter. And really, because I shifted my energy from applying to jobs to looking for clients, things were even scarier. But, you know what? Instead of paralyzing me, fear became the catalyst for how I moved as an entrepreneur. Fear became the fuel for the actions that I took.

The fear of not knowing what to do or having anyone to ask drove me to learn. Fear of not knowing whether I was going to be any good at freelancing pushed me to study other freelancers--their profiles, their portfolios, how they were branding themselves, the prices they were charging, the processes they had in place, etc.--so I could figure out what I should do.

I eventually figured things out. I found clients and started making money. But, the entire process was scary...and to this day, as I evolve and grow my business, things are still scary. There's still fear and uncertainty at times. However, I have learned how to make the fear work for me.

Like I said, fear has become a catalyst for how I move as an entrepreneur. It moves me to action. Once in action, I still operate from a place of fear...but not the scared version of fear, from the F.E.A.R. mindset. F.E.A.R. stands for Face Everything And Rise. So, now, when I am fearful of something, I allow myself some time to feel that emotion and then I make a plan to face everything and rise. I'm not saying that everything always works out as planned, but things always seem to work out--even if it isn't what or how I originally planned or wanted.

To this day, I still experience fear. Sometimes I am able to move past my fears quickly; other times, fear stalls me and I am not able to operate at my best for a short time. But I have learned to recognize when those times are occurring and, even if I don't want to or feel like I can get past it, I push myself into the F.E.A.R. mindset anyway. I put my head down. I dive in. I continue to work. I "face everything and rise" because I realize that whatever I'm fearful about isn't going to go away on its own. It's *my* business. *I* have to be the one to do something about whatever it is I'm afraid of. So, I face that fear.

Is it easier said and done sometimes? Absolutely. But, at the end of the day, what I tell myself is that "failure is not an option." So, I muster through with F.E.A.R. mode in overdrive. And here's the secret to being able to adopt that mentality: I remind myself that I am the one who defines what failure is. For me, failure is doing nothing; it's not trying or giving up because something is hard, not perfect or goes wrong. To me, that's failure. So, anything I do that is more than any of those things is a win.

Does that mean that I take action and everything is suddenly perfect? Absolutely *not*! Being fearless is a process--at least it is for me. Things that used to cause great fear in me when I first became an entrepreneur don't shake me like they used to. Now, they're just part of the journey. And I think that's the key to becoming fearless--understanding that everything *won't* be perfect and that you may have to shift what you're doing or reinvent how you're doing it or who you're doing it for. What it does mean is that I am moving myself from a place of weakness to a place of power because I am taking action.

Taking action builds momentum and when you have momentum, it's much easier to see and experience change. When I see change, my fears are replaced with hope. With hope comes optimism and with optimism comes more action and more change. So, it's the conscious mindset shift from fearful to F.E.A.R. mode that allows me to fear less and to become fearless.

P.S. If you're wondering what happened with the guy, I married him!

CHAPTER TWENTY-SEVEN

Out of My Head

by Whitnie Wiley
Founder/CEO, Shifting Into Action
www.ShiftingIntoAction.now.site

*"Inaction breeds doubt and fear. Action breeds confidence
and courage. If you want to conquer fear, do not sit home and
think about it. Go out and get busy."*
~Dale Carnegie

Were truer words about fear ever spoken? We cannot think our way out of being fearful. And we may not be able to act our way out of it either. While there is technically no such thing as fearless, we can experience fear and take action anyway.

No matter what "mistakes" you've made, no matter where your fear comes from—the voices in your head, the failures of your past—fear is natural and the key is not to have no fear, but to not let fear keep you stuck.

Ask questions. Get curious about why it's popping up. What are you being protected from? Why is there resistance? Resistance is feedback.

Maybe the feedback is not to do things the way you've done them in the past.

That was the nature of my fear. My brain was telling me I'd failed before. If I moved down the path as an entrepreneur, I would fail. As if I needed my brain to remind me. I remembered all too well my short stint at entrepreneurship that sent me screaming back to waiting tables with the clear message I was better off as an employee.

Prior failure is one of the things that creates that inaction Dale Carnegie spoke about—that inability to move. The truth is, however, there is no failure. Either you win or you learn. It took me a long time to observe the patterns in my life of failure, assessment, lesson, adaption, new action. And because it's a pattern, it's something that can be interrupted.

This is my second time around as an entrepreneur. The first time ended in disaster. Okay, disaster is an overstatement, but it's the essence of why I was filled with fear when it came to running my own business.

My first attempt was decades ago when the age of 30 was a stone's throw away and my career was not exactly turning out the way I'd planned or dreamed—with any of my dreams.

From my childhood dreams of being a movie star and model, unfulfilled because I couldn't remember lines, had stage fright and was too short and wide to my desire to become a pediatrician. The doctor dream lasted longer than the model thing, but I ran up against the buzzsaw called organic chemistry. In the end, that career goal also went the way of the dodo, with a new one not solidifying for years.

As I continued with college, the blows kept coming and, one day, I found myself academically dismissed from the university. Being a bit of a rebel, I continued to push forward despite feeling like a failure. I secured jobs, many of which I didn't like, which were mostly reminders that I needed to figure out a way to complete my education or I was going to be in for a life of low-skilled, low pay jobs. Having gone through a divorce and living as a single mother, I was determined not to be a statistic, so finding a better way was my all-consuming goal.

It was in the midst of my failure to get a college degree and figuring out where I was going to go next that I hit the job jackpot. I began working as an engineering technician, a job that could actually lead to a career and one I enjoyed. I remained in that position for three years until learning how politics affected public works projects. The prospect of spending a lifetime working on projects that might not get built had me considering the importance of doing meaningful work. If projects would not be completed, what was the point of expending my time and energy?

By the time these thoughts were floating around in my head, I had met a couple of motivational speakers and the work they were doing intrigued me tremendously. I began revisiting the side of me that embraced helping people. While my work as an engineering tech benefited society as a whole, it didn't have the direct connection that made my heart sing. I had missed that from my days as a tutor.

The more I hung around those people, the more I wanted to be like them and the combination of roadblocking activists and the desire to be more closely connected to my work led me to start the Winner's Edge.

I was young, still willing to take risks and bet on myself, mostly because I didn't know better. With a little more forethought and planning and some studying of what it meant to be an entrepreneur, I probably could have succeeded.

None of that happened. Within short order, the money I had set aside to carry me until I struck it big as a motivational speaker was depleted and I found myself falling behind on my bills. A few months later, I gave in and went to work as a waitress at a then well-known mid-level steakhouse chain. Having worked as a waitress previously, it was not a job I was relishing.

Almost immediately, I found another job as a receptionist for a research library and museum. The beauty of that job was it allowed me to work on ideas I'd begun for the Winner's Edge. Then I got another break. Sort of.

I continued to pitch my ideas as well as apply for jobs. I got an interview with a small privately funded non-profit to run a pilot project. In the interview, most of my time was spent plugging the Winner's Edge as I responded to the questions. Needless to say, I didn't get the job.

A few months later, they hired me to expand the program because they loved my ideas and entrepreneurial spirit. My three years there were heaven and we made an impact on the lives of hundreds of kids, whether they were in the program or not. Making a difference in people's lives through service is in my blood.

Unfortunately, the honeymoon didn't last long as the benefactors of the program decided to relocate and take their money with them. They offered me the opportunity to continue the program, but that required fundraising. By that time, I was in law school looking to create a future in education policy as a way to make sure that all schools had programs like that one. So, I declined.

After an extensive post-graduation job search, I landed a job lobbying for public water agencies. The first couple of years were fine, but the shine of politics, something I'd run away from before, wore off. Once again, I found myself unhappy in my work.

However, unlike other times in my life when my tolerance and patience were short and jumping ship seemed like the best option, this time I couldn't pull the trigger. As badly as I wanted out, I wasn't getting hired by anyone else and I didn't have the nerve to simply quit. Which turned out was the best thing for me.

Not only was I disillusioned with politics, but my employer was pretty dysfunctional. As I observed the toxicity from every angle, I grew curious about why organizational dysfunction and poor leadership existed, which drove me to get degrees in organizations and leadership.

While I was in school, I completed a coaching certification program, which opened my eyes about what was going on with me: One) by that time I was already coaching clients and the certification, while helpful, wasn't necessary; Two) adding the additional degrees was more about delaying taking action; and Three) even after completing the certification and degrees, I still delayed leaving my job. I was afraid and I wasn't necessarily looking to be an entrepreneur.

All of that was fear based. I took the job out of fear of not getting what I wanted. Then I stayed because I didn't have the nerve to leave. Day after day, however, I felt as if my soul was being sucked out of me and knew changes had to be made. But I was paralyzed with fear from all the failures that had piled up in my past.

As the misery I was experiencing from work crept into my personal life and in particular my marriage, I knew I had to make changes. I followed these steps that you can take, too.

1) Give yourself permission to feel what you feel.
2) Confirm your safety.
3) Recognize that the fear is not only natural, but okay.
4) Remember that mistakes are part of the process and are opportunities to learn.
5) Focus on your past successes.
6) Be okay with not having all the answers.
7) Decide to take, then take action.

While I am not the biggest risk taker, my entrepreneurial journey is about feeling the fear and doing it anyway. Whether fearless or fearful, the bottom line is to take action.

CHAPTER TWENTY-EIGHT

Network Marketing Saved My Life

by Will Zanders
Director, Southern Summit Consulting, LLC
www.MakeMLMGreatAgain.com

Network Marketing saved my life. Literally.

"What?" you ask, rubbing your ear. "Did I hear you right?" It's true.

My story starts in uptown New Orleans. Both my parents had college degrees. All I heard growing up was how important going to college was, "Get that degree, Will. Land a steady job with a good paycheck, health benefits, and a retirement plan. That's the path to a happy life." It never occurred to me to notice that we lived paycheck to paycheck in a Welfare neighborhood.

Still, I listened. I busted my ass, got the grades, went to college, and then to law school, and BOOM, landed a prestigious job offer with a highly respected firm. After all, being a lawyer is right up there with being a doctor, right? Prestige, honor, and most of all, money.

So why then did I still have to side hustle as a personal trainer just to make ends meet?

During that time, I tried to get a business going. The problem was that it seemed like every business I attempted flopped. I just couldn't get things going. And I tried every scam and scheme in the book – legitimate or not.

I worked myself to the point of exhaustion and finally made the choice to dump lawyering and join the police force. Now I was in it, just like my parents wanted: solid job, steady paycheck, great benefits, and a full retirement plan. And I discovered I was good at being a cop. I was talented. It wasn't long before I was working in undercover narcotics.

But here's the thing: my life was not good. I worked ALL the time. Cops work long shifts, and undercover is no picnic. It's seedy and dangerous and extremely high stress. Four out of five cops I personally knew got shot or shot at while on the job. It was only a matter of time until it happened to me. I mean, at 6'4" I'm a big target – hard to miss. I had no desire to die because some scumbag decided to use me for human target practice.

Worse still, I had to spend my weekends on my side hustle. This is not a good situation for a family. I ended up divorced, broke, and once again living paycheck to paycheck.

Meanwhile, it was not all peaches and cream for my family. My father's health was declining, and one day, he fainted dead away into my arms. We called 911, terrified and panicked. What was happening here? He was admitted to the hospital, and after days of running tests, the doctor informed us that he was "suffering from a form of kidney cancer and the numbers were not life sustaining."

A dire prognosis indeed.

In the midst of this, this kid who was a bagger at the grocery store where I shopped tried to tell me about his network marketing gig. His excitement was contagious, and I jumped at the chance, in spite of the calamitous warnings from my mom, my dad, my brothers, my aunt, my cousins… pretty much everyone… that network marketing was a scam and a scheme.

Not a scam, I thought, *an opportunity.*

In the first six months, I cleared six figures. SIX FIGURES.

I was floored. This was beyond my wildest dreams. I'd never experienced that kind of money. I just knew I wanted it to continue. So, at age 35, I "retired" from the police force, joined the ranks of the happily unemployed, committed myself fully to my business, and never looked back. I became a student of the network marketing business model and absorbed everything I could to learn more. I was, and still am, absolutely hooked on the simplicity and brilliance of it.

Yes, in the beginning, I did make sacrifices. But here's the thing: I knew that all the effort I invested would pay off on the back end, when I could relax and let all my hard work pay off. I knew that I was sowing seeds that would grow and bloom later. I think that's something entrepreneurs instinctively understand and that leads them to pursue their dreams.

I did have one bump in the network marketing road when the company I was a part of folded under the weight of bankruptcy. So, I did my research. In the summer of 2019, I jumped to a solid company that I could believe in. After all, if I was going to dedicate myself to promoting something, I wanted it to be the best. What did I choose? Heart & Body Naturals (HBN). The added bonus: they are great about training the newbies. They offer tons of support and training because they get that your success is essential to their success. I love a good win-win-win: the company wins, I win, and my customers win.

As my success grew, my parents took an interest in the success that the HBN products were having with my customers. They decided to take some steps toward their own health and began using the HBN products. Wonder of wonders, they liked them! Not only did they like them, they were inspired to begin a healthier regimen of eating well, exercising, and just generally taking better care of themselves.

Now, a couple years later, my father's health has improved to the point where his doctors have taken him off ALL his medications. He is brimming with good health. He has the energy to indulge his love of travelling hundreds of miles every week to see his grandchildren and is currently writing his third book.

And my mother? Why, she joined HBN herself! She has set up a nifty little side biz that earns her a nice extra income to supplement their retirement AND provides them with some mad money for the fun stuff.

The shift in my family is the coolest thing ever. My naysaying parents no longer think I'm crazy. They now know this is no scheme – no scam. In fact, they became big fans when I purchased a house for them... and then paid off my father's car. One of the coolest benefits of my new lifestyle is that I get to provide for my loved ones; everything from necessities to fun trips.

Life. Is. Good.

You may think I say that network marketing saved my life because I have achieved the lifestyle I wanted, with enough money to live very comfortably. But that isn't the thing that saved me.

It's this: exactly two weeks to the day after I "retired" from the police force, the man who replaced me in the department was shot twice while on the job.

He had stepped into my job. My exact position. If I hadn't left when I did, it would have been me there in that decrepit home, facing down a lunatic with a gun. It would have been me with two bullets in my chest.

It would have been me.

My heart goes out to that cop and his family. I hug my loved ones closer and give gratitude every day because of that man's sacrifice.

Now I share my story to inspire others who are unhappy or dissatisfied or underpaid to step up and take the reins of their own lives.

Think about this: if you invest all the effort and time into building your own network marketing biz as you currently invest into your "stable job," how fast could you earn your first six figures?

I'm betting on six months.

Contributor Biographies

The contributors would love to hear from you! For a link to contact them, go to:

www.TheFearlessEntrepreneurs.com

 **Lynda Sunshine West** is known as The Fear Buster. She's a Speaker, 6 Time Bestselling Author, in 3 categories of success, Mastermind Facilitator, Executive Film Producer, Red Carpet Interviewer, and the Founder of Women Action Takers. At age 51 she faced one fear every day for an entire year. In doing so, she gained an exorbitant amount of confidence and uses what she learned by facing a fear every day to fulfill her mission of helping 5 million women entrepreneurs gain the confidence to share their voice with the world. Her collaboration books, mastermind, podcast, and many more opportunities give women from all over the world the opportunity to share their voice with the world. She believes in cooperation and collaboration and loves connecting with like-minded people.

You can connect with Lynda Sunshine here: WomenActionTakers.com.

Erik "Mr. Awesome" Swanson is an award winning International Keynote Speaker, 10 Time #1 National Best-Selling Author in 5 different categories of success, Erik "Mr. Awesome" Swanson is in great demand around the world! Speaking on average to more than one million people per year, and honored to be invited to speak to Business and Entrepreneurial school of Harvard University as well as joining the Ted Talk Family with his latest TEDx speech called "A Dose of Awesome."

You can easily find Erik sharing stages with some of the most talented and famous speakers of the world, such as Brian Tracy, Nasa's Performance Coach Dr. Denis Waitley, from the book & movie 'The Secret,' Bob Proctor, Jack Canfield, John Assaraf, Millionaire Maker Loral Langemeier, Co-Author of 'Rich Dad Poor Dad,' Outwitting the Devil, Three Feet from Gold, and Exit Rich, Sharon Lechter, Legendary Motivator Les Brown, among many others!

Mr. Swanson has created and developed the super popular Habitude Warrior Conference which has a 2-year waiting list and includes 33 top named speakers, all in a 'Ted Talk' style event which has quickly climbed as one of the top 10 events not to miss in the United States! Erik's motto is clear: "NDSO!" No Drama – Serve Others! He has also created his Habitude Warrior Special Edition Book Series called 13 Steps to Riches which includes 13 powerhouse, famous celebrity authors as well as 33 up and coming bestselling authors and leaders.

You can connect with Mr. Awesome here: SpeakerErikSwanson.com.

Dennis Haber is an entrepreneur, attorney, author, speaker, Ziglar Legacy Certified Trainer/ Coach, and DISC Certified Behavior Consultant. His book, Don't Play with Fire, is helping people live as if they are living life for a second time, but this time smarter and wiser.

He also is a contributing author in the bestselling book MOMENTUM where you learn how to capitalize on one of the greatest forces known to mankind.

You can connect with Dennis here: www.DennisHaber.com.

Alice Pallum, the founder and CEO of AMP Enterprises, LTD, spent 17 years in corporate America. After her job was eliminated, she started her own consulting/coaching business. She has an incredible story to tell.

You can connect with Alice here: www.ampbusinesscoaching.com

Amy Edge, CEO + Founder of Amy Edge & CO, is an operations and project management strategist who has spent many years working with true visionaries and creatives in the online and digital space. She has honed her skills as an operational leader and partners with her clients as their Certified Director of Operations and integrator within their business.

Through this strategic partnership, she manages & creates operations that increase profits, empower their team, and scale their business without frustration and complete ease. As Amy supports these coaches and creatives they are able to fully step into their CEO role & bring their ultimate vision of business success to fruition.

You can connect Amy here: www.AmyEdge.com.

Amy Lee Kaiser, LMT, Author, Reiki Master, Pelvis Wellness Warrior, is the owner of Soul Healing Bodywork & Wellness Center. She is passionate about empowering women to heal themselves and guiding them to their own feminine power. She is a gifted healer and self-proclaimed Pelvis Wellness Warrior.

Amy's daughter and two sons are her biggest teachers, supporters and motivation to do her work. "They help me see what is truly important and make me incredibly proud of them AND of myself, for raising that caliber of human."

You can connect with Amy here: www.SoulHealingBodyworkWellnessCenter.com.

Andy Nam, Director of Foco Research LLC, is a functional nutritionist and personal trainer specializing in helping people live longer lives with optimum health. His unique approach helps his clients get into the best shape of their life.

He is also the author of the forthcoming book Live Long and Thrive. He lives with his wife Minna and four cats in Texas where they enjoy all the fun activities that he was unable to do as a young man.

You can connect with Andy here: www.FocoAcademy.com.

Bhakti Ishaya was born and raised on a farm in southeast Minnesota. He attended three different high schools, and three different colleges in different states. After he got out of the Army, he was in the hospitality industry for seven years in four different states, was president and CEO of a Minnesota-based national company, and worked as a consultant for a variety of companies.

Bhakti is now a full-time monk with an international organization called The Bright Path and is in his sixth year of teaching Ascension, which is an effective inner practice. He and most others experience it as being beyond meditation. Bhakti, like many others, have found that an effective inner practice leads to abundance in all areas of one's life. For example: two of Bhakti's students have published books, and three others have expanded their organizations internationally. They, as well as others, have found peace in their endeavors.

You can connect with Bhakti here: www.TheBrightPath.com.

Brandon Straza is the Founder and President of The Success Finder, an App dedicated to supporting Coach/Member relationships through direct communication, Mastermind offerings, networking, and support. An entrepreneur before it was trendy, Brandon has built up a number of successful businesses, serves as President and Owner of American Option Insurance, and produces a weekly podcast. Brandon, his wife, Angela, and their son, Liam, live in Dallas, TX.

You can connect with Brandon here: www.TheSuccessFinder.com.

David Smith is a Certified Entrepreneurship and Business Coach with a focus on Money Mindset Transformation. After being a six-figure seller on Amazon, he started the From Debt to Wealth to Impact Podcast because most people have too much debt and too little and too little saved for retirement.

His mission is to help people profit from their passion and start a home business in six weeks. David is also a proud Desert Storm U.S. Air Force Veteran.

You can connect with David here: www.DavidSmithSpeaks.com.

Elizabeth Moors is an Aspie and a parent of a successful teenage son with Aspergers. She helps parents raise their child with Aspergers/HFA to be independent & successful. She is a Certified John Maxwell trainer as well as certified in NLP, REBT, and EI. Elizabeth is a 3x bestselling author.

Her first book is titled *Taking Charge of You: Raising An Independent & Successful Child With Aspergers.*

You can connect with Elizabeth here: www.ElizabethMoors.com.

Kohila Sivas is a parent, teacher, Math Intervention-ist, Holistic and NLP Success Coach for students and parents. Over the past 22 years, Kohila has developed a simple, proven system called MathCodes and she uses this system to help students rapidly transform their math performance as well as shift their mind-set, grow their confidence, and outperform their expectations in all areas of their life. She also certifies other teachers and tutors to use her proven MathCodes system.

You can connect with Kohila here: www.mathcodes.com.

Kristy Boyd Johnson is the Boss Lady at Turtle Sea Books. She is the author of more than 30 books, holds an MFA in Screenwriting, is a recovering school teacher, and loves writing children's books. Her favorite pastimes are swimming, long walks, and reading a great book.

You can connect with Kristy here:www.TurtleSea-Books.com.

Simply put, **Krystylle Richardson** loves seeing people become better versions of themselves mentally, physically, spiritually, financially, emotionally and more. Krystylle believes that she was personally put on this earth by God to help people evict mind-trash and cancel mediocrity. She played small in portions of her life for years. That feeling sucked, so she did something about it. She believes that we all have greatness and we can activate God's favor if we just move out of our own way.

Krystylle's focus is helping women as a Wealth Innovation Coach. She helps them identify their real purpose, increase streams of income and media exposure so they can Be Heard, Be Great & Get Paid.

She is the energized creator of The Woman Weekend-Preneur™ and is the ICN Global Ambassador of Innovation. Krystylle has 35 years of experience in international business. Her faith and unique skillsets have produced countless testimonials and her being given the name "The Untapped Income Coach."

Krystylle is an International Speaker - Leadership and Mindset Account-ability Coach - International Bestselling Author - TV & Radio Show Host - Red Carpet Interviewer - Philanthropist - an Awarded Humanitarian - Missionary - Genetic Research Engineer & Exec - Wife and Mother.

She has been featured in USA Today, NBC, CBS, Think & Grow Rich Legacy World Tour, Hollywood Glam and coming soon in Yahoo! Finance. She believes that after self-acceptance, she knows for a fact that the possibilities are endless. Krystylle's superpower is RELENTLESS TENACITY and living out loud.

You can connect with Krystylle here: www.KrystylleRichardson.com.

Kym Glass is a Soft Skills Consultant, TEDx & Award-Winning Speaker, and four-time Bestselling Author.

With 20+ years of corporate and 18 years of entrepreneur and business owner experience, Kym works with organizations, individuals, and teams to leverage Soft Skills Strategies for Bottom-Line Results.

As the author of her personal story, Unshakeable Courage, she shares the true story of her escape from a religious cult to help others overcome their own self-limiting fear.

As a natural connector, Kym is always passionate to learn more about her client's business to understand where unshakeable courage can create sales and teams that soar.

Kym Glass is available for speaking engagements, interviews, and corporate live and Zoom® events. To book Kym Glass or for more information on soft skills, speaking, and publishing brilliance visit www.KymGlass.com.

Lois Koffi is the Founder of Lois Koffi Enterprises. She is a professional speaker with thousands of speeches under her belt to inspire, educate and empower speakers, authors, entrepreneurs/salespeople to be the best version of themselves.

She has coached thousands of people in business and lifestyle. She went from a six-figure salary and a dream team to nothing at all and bounced back stronger than ever. She is now serving people all over the world and teaching them how to step into their greatness.

You can connect with Lois here: www.LoisKoffi.com.

Lola Oyafemi mentors powerful coaches who want to leverage social media to attract and close dream clients without cold pitching, bro-marketing, or slimy techniques.

You can connect with Lola here: www.LolaOyafemi.com.

Marilen Crump is the founder of ARTINSPIRED, LLC (EST 2000), Creator of the $1k in a Day Program™, and President of the Phenomenal Female Business Network™ where the mission is to help women develop their passions, grow their audience, achieve business milestones, and fund their dreams. Marilen loves to serve Creatives and Dreamers and is on a mission to help as many entrepreneurs develop strong business plans and monetize their passions. Her clients are experiencing success with the ability to book $20K Clients and create recurring revenue through platforms that Marilen has helped them to brand and develop. She has been featured on International Virtual Summits, Economic Development Conferences, College Campus Events and as a Commencement Speaker, and prominent organizations such as NASA and Civitan International. She thrives in spaces where people are playing BIG – and – getting YOU Ready to Step into the Next Level is her passion.

You can connect with Marilen here: https://MarilenCump.com.

Mark Ledlow is a United States Marine Corps Veteran. He has worked in Juvenile Corrections and as a Reserve Police Officer. After 10 years in Corporate America, Mark Launched Ledlow Security Group and Founded Fearless Mindset Podcast.

You can connect with Mark at www.FearlessMindsetPodcast.com.

Mary Elizabeth Jackson is the 2017 Gold Maxy award-winning author of the children's book series *Perfectly Precious Poohlicious, Poohlicious Look at Me,* and *Poohlicious Oh the Wonder of Me* (Tuscany Bay Books). *Cheers from Heaven,* a mid-grade reader releases late 2021 (Tuscany Bay Books), with co-writer Thornton Cline. Jackson focuses on writing empowering books for kids. Jackson is also a ghostwriter, book collaborator, and the voice for the Sports2Gether app.

Mrs. Jackson is a special needs advocate and an Ambassador Advocate for AutismTn. She co-founded and co-hosts Writers Corner Live TV and Special Needs TV Shows that air on Amazon Live, Facebook, Twitter, LinkedIn, and YouTube. Writers Corner Live features author interviews and all things in the writing world. Special Needs TV features interviews and resources for parents, families, and caregivers. Jackson is also working on an edutainment YouTube channel with her son featuring children's book reviews and family fun and education.

You can connect with Mary here: www.MaryEJackson.com.

As an overthinking, fearful, waiting-for-the-right-time perfectionist, **Missy Holder** discovered the "secret" to chasing her dreams and achieving her goals... to take imperfect action and chase her dreams DESPITE her fears! She coaches and empowers women to take imperfect action toward their goals so they, too, can live purposeful, rewarding lives of their dreams and transform into the best version of themselves in the process.

You can connect with Missy here: www.MissyHolder.com.

Mistie Layne is an Empowerment and Resiliency expert transforming lives by helping release toxic beliefs to overcome any adversity with confidence and resilience. Mistie overcame her worst to live her best by realizing her past was robbing her future and decided to take control of her own life. She is now a bestselling author of her life story, *What Goes Up*, and claims writing was the therapy that saved her life while sitting in a prison facing a forty-year sentence. When you learn more about Mistie, you will be inspired to adopt a positive mentality by realizing you are now an authority on the other side of your adversity and can use your knowledge to help others.

You can connect with Mistie here: www.StepUpAndSpeakOut.com.

Monica Allen is a serial entrepreneur owning several businesses. She is co-owner of Allen Professional Graphics Group (APGG) dba Zeus' Closet, stuff4GREEKS & FratBrat, and Deuce Equity Group. She is the sole proprietor of Monica Allen Interiors and Stitched for Success. She believes that being surrounded by positive people, believing in yourself, and having faith in God has led to her success.

Monica majored in Risk Management and Insurance at the University of Georgia and earned her MBA from Georgia State University. After working in Corporate America for 8 years, Monica left her full-time job to pursue her entrepreneurial goals. Having started APGG while working full time, the company had grown and required full-time attention. Later she began studying interior design at SCAD. Monica also co-authored *You've Graduated. Now What? 10 Steps to Stand Out and Get Hired in the New Economy.*

Starting a podcast called Stitched for Success in 2020, Monica is dedicated to teaching business and life lessons to help aspiring and ambitious entrepreneurs and serious side hustlers launch, grow and scale your business while avoiding many of the pitfalls of running your own company.

She is a wife, daughter, and mom of two.

You can connect with Monica here: www.StitchedForSuccess.com.

Sally Green is the founder of The Self-Care Rockstar, empowering people to begin a regime of self-care for healthy living. She is a Christian educator, artist, and a 2-time international bestselling author. Sally has also written two Bible studies and an inspirational book of poetry.

You can connect with Sally here: www.TheSelfCareRockstar.com.

Shanna Lee Moore is the owner of Developing True Health and Justice Massage, hydration consultant, educator, entrepreneur, writer and poet. She lives in Southern California with her family. Her mission is to empower others to create the life they've always wanted.

You can connect with Shanna here: www.developingtruehealth.com.

Sherri Leopold is a mentor, 3 times International Bestselling Author, Speaker, Founder and CEO of Dream Big with Sherri Leopold. She is a Dr. Amen Licensed Brain Health Trainer and enjoys teaching on the topic of brain health. She is a television host of the show *Outside the Box with Sherri Leopold* on Legrity.TV. She has worked in the Network Marketing/Direct Selling industry as a top producer for 24 years, sharing her expertise in speaking, mentoring, and team building.

Sherri released her first book in June of 2019 called Self-Bullying: What To Do When the Bully is YOU! As Leader of the Stop Self-Bullying Movement, Sherri has a membership program called War On Words (WOW) Warriors. This Stop Self-Bullying training helps eradicate negative self-talk and teaches people to Stand UP and Stand OUT as the unrepeatable miracle they are!! She has designed a Facebook support group called WOW Warriors to encourage self-love and create a place of love and encouragement.

You can connect with Sherri here: www.SherriLeopold.com.

Tanisha Coffey is a seasoned entrepreneur with 15+ years under her belt. The Detroit, Michigan, native began her entrepreneurial journey as a freelance copywriter/ghostwriter and marketing consultant. She later formed her first LLC. As her business continued to evolve, Coffey's The Lofty Entrepreneur brand was born.

Through The Lofty Entrepreneur brand, Tanisha assists current and aspiring entrepreneurs by providing business coaching, tips, tools, advice, and resources to help them to start, launch and grow their business. She is also the author of *30-Minute Startup: A Step-by-Step Guide For Setting Up Your Business Legally* and *$100 Bucks Branding: Branding Your Business On A Shoestring Budget*. In addition to being a business coach and author, Tanisha is a speaker and the creator of the 7-Day Business Launch Intensive.

Tanisha currently lives in Central Florida with her husband and children.

You can connect with Tanisha here: www.TheLoftyEntrepreneur.com.

After the death of her son and finding it difficult to say out loud much of what she was experiencing, **Whitnie Wiley**'s journey as an author began by her chronicling her grief journey.

Since those painful early days, Whitnie has shared her words on leadership and career management with hundreds of thousands of readers around the world as the author for the Lead the Way column in the Association of Corporate Counsel's Docket magazine. She encouraged her readers to develop self-awareness and use their values and priorities to pave their path to enjoying their careers, better leadership, and improved teamwork.